The Duellist's

Duellist's

Companion

A training manual for 17th century Italian rapier

Guy Windsor

The School of European Swordsmanship, Helsinki

The Duellist's Companion
A training manual for 17th century Italian rapier

Guy Windsor

Published in Finland and the United States

Copyright © 2012 Guy Windsor & The School of European Swordsmanship Oy

ISBN: 978-952-67934-4-3 (paperback)

Book design by Ilkka Hartikainen

Windsor, Guy (1973—)

Contents

For
My wife Michaela,

And in memory of my grandfather
Dr. Hector D. Apergis (1895—1987)
who showed me that swords, bows and guns
are not toys for children but the proper
accoutrements of a gentleman.

About the Author

Guy Windsor has been studying swordsmanship and other martial arts since about 1985, and the rapier since about 1993. In 1994 he co-founded the Dawn Duellists Society, one of the first British societies for the study of western martial arts. He graduated from Edinburgh University with an MA (Hons) in 1996, and worked as a cabinet-maker and antiques restorer for five years. He then moved to Helsinki, Finland and opened The School of European Swordsmanship. He has been teaching historical swordsmanship full-time ever since. Since 2001 the school has grown to five branches in Finland, and there are two groups in Sweden and one in Singapore training under his direction. His first book, *The Swordsman's Companion*, was published in 2004, and quickly became the standard work on Italian longsword.

Introduction

The rapier is arguably the most romantic of all European swords. In history, fiction, and on the screen, the rapier has been carried and used by dashing heroes and vicious villains for defence, murder, and swashbuckling adventure. If it was good enough for d'Artagnan, the Admirable Chrichton, and Cyrano de Bergerac, it's surely good enough for us ordinary mortals.

It is unsurprising then that it is one of the most popular choices for modern students of the sword, be they historical swordsmanship researchers, re-enactors, SCA fencers, or live-roleplayers. Four feet of glistening steel, with an intricate hilt has undeniable attraction.

My own interest in the weapon is primarily practical: I really enjoy fencing with it.

I have been playing with rapiers for about a dozen years; coming from a sport-fencing background, I was inclined to use the weapon like a very large foil; this met with only limited success. I soon figured out that I needed some better ideas about how to use it. A little digging soon produced a plethora of how-to books written between about 1570 and 1670 that could tell me how it should be done, if only I could work out the language: either archaic English (not so bad) or Italian (much harder). It soon appeared that the one book that all authorities seemed to talk about (such as Gaugler, Castle, and Hutton) was the *Gran Simulacro* of Ridolfo Capo Ferro, published in 1610. This seemed the logical place to start.

However, my research into Capo Ferro did not take off in earnest until I attended Maestro Sean Hayes' class on the subject at Benecia in June 2003. His class, though only a few hours long, was the key that unlocked the hitherto closed door of the treatise for me. A few months later, I met Jherek Swanger (in another of Mro. Hayes' classes, this time in Lansing), and from

1

him obtained a copy of the translation of the whole treatise that he and William Wilson had produced. My own Italian skills were sufficient for me to have plodded through a few sections, but Bill and Jherek's work dramatically speeded up my progress, to the point where it was a productive use of my time. This book is therefore in large measure a tribute to their hard work and expertise. Gentlemen, many thanks.

This book is designed to offer a working training method based on an original historical fencing source. It is intended to be not only a guide for a beginner wishing to learn rapier fencing, but also an example for other researchers for how such a method can be created from the source material.

The original Source

Ridolfo Capo Ferro's amazing work, *Il Gran Simulacro dell'arte e dell'uso della scherma* ("the great representation of the art and use of fencing") first published in 1610 is perhaps the most famous fencing treatise ever written, and in its time went through many editions. It contains within it enough instruction for a complete method of fencing to be derived from it. However, the original language (Italian) is unknown to many aspiring rapier fencers, and the style of the text can make it difficult for a beginner to work out what exactly the instructions are telling you to do. In addition, there is a significant gap between working through the set drills laid down by Capo Ferro, and actually free-fencing using his style.

There is also the consideration of completeness. In this book, there is not the scope to go through every single play contained in Capo Ferro's masterwork; neither does *Gran Simulacro* contain every possible correct rapier play. A brief scan through a few contemporary works, such a Giganti's *Scola* (1606)[1] or Fabris' *Scienza*[2] will show techniques that do not appear in *Gran Simulacro*, yet clearly work. When writing a manual, it is impossible to be entirely comprehensive, so what is contained in *Gran Simulacro* is not the complete repertoire of correct rapier technique, but one master's selection of representative techniques drawn from a larger body of possible options. Your guide through those options (including the ones he left out, but which appear in other manuals), is the fencing theory that Capo Ferro's method is based on, and which he clearly expended a lot of effort and ink to describe. I have attempted in this book to analyse the reasons behind every action, and have selected the actions and sequences that I think illustrate those reasons most clearly.

Capo Ferro's treatise is divided into a *Tavola Generale dell'arte della scherma* ("General Table of the Art of Fencing"), *Alcuni Ricordi, o vero avertimenti della scherma* ("Some Admonitions, or Advice, on Fencing"), *Dichiaratione d'alcuni termini della scherma* ("Explanations of Some Terms of Fencing"), and the Plates, a series of two page spreads, one page with an illustration, and its facing page with the explanatory text. The Table is subdivided into 13 named chapters, and 118 numbered paragraphs (for example chapter 11 contains paragraphs 104 to 111). The "Admonitions" are 13 named and numbered paragraphs; the "Explanations" comprise 17 numbered paragraphs. The plates are numbered from 1 to 43. At the end of the treatise are two further short chapters, *D'Alcuni Termini del taglio* ("Of Some Terms of the Cut") and *Modo Sicuro de difendersi da ogni sorte di colpi* ("A Secure way to Defend Oneself From Every Sort of Blow"). The General Table comprises the "Art" of fencing; the Admonitions, Explanations and the Plates comprise the "Use", as mentioned in the title. This distinction between Art and Use is crucially important; as Capo Ferro puts it:

> There is the greatest difference between the art and the use, and perchance not less than between reason and luck, between confusion and good order, between knowledge and opinion[3] (**Admonitions, first paragraph**)

He goes on to say:

> Truth commands the art, ... those precepts that do not stand as paragons of their laws are not recognized as theirs. The use of the art encompasses much more, and considers not only the true things, but cautions us also of the false and of the many other particular details that variously occur; and in order to show its effects, takes advantage of the aid of many disciplines. (**Admonitions, first paragraph**)

In other words, we must distinguish between theory and practice; the ideal, fundamentally true and hence always reliable perfect Art, and the more mundane, "do what works" Use. At times, apparent contradictions in the text[4], are often resolved if you take into account whether they are referring to the ideal "Art" or the practical "Use". The ideal sword fight never happens; understanding the "Art" will help you apply your skill effectively when your opponent does something unexpected.

I have tried to support every statement with reference to the text. The pagination in the 1610 edition is inconsistent to the point of being misleading and unusable, and in any case not very informative or precise. So instead I refer to the sections from which I am drawing my conclusions by the section's name and the paragraph number, or the plate number, or the chapter name. So for example, "Admonitions 12" refers to the twelfth paragraph of the "Admonitions" section; "plate 7" refers either to the text accompanying plate 7, or the picture itself.

It is my hope that once you have worked through this book, you will be inspired to go back to the original, and work through every play from every plate, and enthusiastically peruse the theory sections to deepen your understanding of the basis of the art. In the course of this research you will no doubt encounter points where you are forced to disagree with something I say here. Remember, when in doubt, believe the chap who faced death by stabbing if he made a mistake. Original sources always take precedence over modern interpretations.

I will assume that the reader has no knowledge of the original source, nor any fencing experience, and attempt to teach the style from the ground up.

A link in a chain

The *Gran Simulacro* was published in 1610. It is in many ways the perfect example of the modern method for teaching a weapon style: theory, followed by a few (usually numbered) postures, or guards, a very few basic actions and movements (the lunge, the stringere, etc.), and then a great number of sequences comprising various preparations, attacks and counters. In essence, there are a few positions, and many techniques.

This is an astounding contrast to the earlier methodology, in use from at least as early as 1400 (see *Flos Duellatorum* by Fiore de' Liberi, written in 1409), and still being used in the late sixteenth century, of encoding a fencing system by the use of named positions.

This method of structuring a system, employed by all the masters of the Bolognese school (Achille Marozzo is the most famous), was as far as we can tell from the existing record of treatises, absolutely general in Italy until the advent of Agrippa (who published his seminal work on fencing in 1553) and Viggiani (who wrote *Lo Schermo* in about 1550, though it was not published until 1575).

Viggiani's methodology is closely related to the "guards" method, in that he encodes all techniques by positions, though he rejects the standard names and instead defines each position, and numbers it. So Viggiani's method of teaching the rising cut from the left is to define the start position (first ward), and the end position (second ward), and he states "between two blows lies a guard, between two guards lies a blow".

Agrippa, on the other hand, merely defines four guards by the position of the hand (a terminology that has remained in fencing usage to the present)[5], and proceeds to describe a number of techniques that may be done from the guards.

Capo Ferro follows Agrippa's lead, in that he (as all fencers did from then on) all but abandons the old-style use of named guards (there are a few mentions of such positions at the end of the book, but none are defined, and no real use is made of them), and simply shows basic ready positions (six, because the use of the dagger requires a couple of extras) and things to be done from them.

What occasioned this transition cannot be stated with any certainty, but one may observe that it came about when the weapon in use shifted from a largely cut-oriented sword, with military applicability, to a thrust-oriented weapon, of practically no military value. The legions of cut-oriented fencing manuals that appear after the latter method was firmly established suggest that it is the context in which the weapon was taught and used, not the weapon itself, which led to the change. For the first time in history, a purely civilian fencing system was being developed, and so a method perfectly suited for drilling squads of soldiers (I can hear myself in the salle, when teaching longsword, barking "fenestra!" "longa!", "chinghiale!" like a drill sergeant) gave way to a method better adapted for individual instruction.

It is important to realise that Capo Ferro was not writing in a fencing vacuum; he represents a particularly distinguished link in a chain, but a link nonetheless.

Historical Fencing

What is historical fencing? In my opinion, historical fencing describes the process of analysing historical documents (usually treatises on fencing), deriving fencing instruction from them, and then drilling those fencing actions until one can fence in a manner that an informed observer would be able to identify as the style of a given source. The ultimate test of a historical fencer specialising in Capo Ferro would be to go back in time to Capo Ferro's fencing salle in 1610, and to have his fencing style recognised by the master as his own.

There are usually multiple historical sources for any given weapon. There are literally dozens available for the rapier. Most historical fencers do choose to fill in gaps apparent in one style with material borrowed from another. This is often necessary, and in no way invalidates the "historicity" of the fencer's style, provided that the fencer makes only valid borrowings, and is aware of his sources.

Research is a never ending process of development. I doubt there will ever come a time when I will be able to say with confidence "this is exactly Capo Ferro's method". However, there comes a point when the basic framework is clear, and the basic concepts understood if not mastered. My colleagues and I may be arguing about the precise hand position when in the guard *"terza"* for the next ten years; but we can execute the sequences that require such a guard, and have them work in the way described by the text. That is enough to be going on with. Further research, though interesting, and vital for the long-term good of the Art, starts entering the area of diminishing returns. I suspect that some of the interpretations in this book will change with further breakthroughs, but I believe that we have enough of the big picture filled in to make fencing "Capo Ferro style rapier" possible. We must strike a balance between the pure researcher's absolute insistence on every detail being exact, and the purely practical "well, this works for me" approach.

This raises the question of why train in an interpreted system when that interpretation may change? Is all the time spent training in early, incorrect interpretations wasted? My students are now accustomed to me finding out new things (often from one of them), and incorporating the new idea into the training system. The core of my approach is to work on understanding the tactical and biomechanical reasons for doing any technique in a particular way. Every choice is a compromise between stability and mobility, attacking capability and defensive capability, each specific to the weapon used, the tactical situation, and the prevailing cultural expectations. The system under discussion makes radically different choices to, for example, Fiore's medieval combat system for the longsword, because the weapon is radically different, and the context in which it is used is radically different.

5

I do not teach my students to lunge like this just because "that's how Capo Ferro tells us to do it". How I think Capo Ferro tells us to do it may change. I first analyse *why* I think Capo Ferro has us do it this way, and then teach it according to the tactical and mechanical principles underlying the action. I try to explain wherever possible the compromises being made and the rationale behind these compromises. This way, should the interpretation change, my students are taught a different set of compromises, rather than "that was wrong. Now do it this way". Instead, I'll tell them "I think Capo Ferro is actually making these choices, so we will now do it this way".

The interpretation may have been wrong, but the analysis of the compromises, if accurate, was clearly sensible. One of the most common corrections a student will hear from me is "that's wrong for this weapon. So do it like *so*". Many of the really common mistakes my beginners make with the rapier are actually correct actions for another weapon.

In effect, by studying the mechanical and tactical principles of a martial art, rather than just learning its techniques, we learn to adapt to new interpretations very fast, and can still make the old interpretations work when necessary.

The very fact that we are training a researched martial art, instead of an inherited one, meaning that we will have to constantly update our interpretation, is a good thing. It requires us to study more deeply the fundamental principles at play behind the technical choices being made.

However, if all you want to do is win fights, then the approach should be different. Pick a system that suits your way of thinking and your body type, and train the basic techniques until you are incapable of moving outside the system. Then fight a lot, and learn to apply the basics you have internalised. Don't expect this way to lead to understanding, but it is the best way to acquire defensive skills. Military drill instructors don't discuss the structure of the elbow joint when teaching close-quarter fighting; they just make you do a few techniques over and over until they work. When attacked, the student just reacts as he has been taught. No thought, no choices.

I have no interest in training people to kill each other. The glory and strength of this Art is that it has outlived its street usefulness. In Capo Ferro's terms, we may candidly focus on the Art, not the Use. There is no immediate need to prove our art by combat. While it is essential to test ourselves and our understanding of the Art in earnest competitive bouts, there is no hurry to get there: none of my students need the Art to save their lives next week, next year, or, hopefully, ever. So we have the luxury of training for the love of it, for the Art's own sake. This brings us to a very different place; ultimately, the ability to make graceful, artistic choices under extreme pressure.

Using this book

Capo Ferro lays out his *Gran Simulacro* beginning with a general intro-
duction, then defining his terms and explaining the theory of fencing he uses,
before showing basic guards, the lunge, the stringere, and then a whole
sequence of plays. This is perhaps the ideal structure for an explanatory book
on a topic that everyone has some basic background in, and it is the structure
I chose for my first book, *The Swordsman's Companion*. However, here I have
decided to interweave the theory and practical applications because I have
found that in my classes the students grasp the theory better when the
application or physical manifestation is immediately presented.

So, to make the best use of this book, please read it from start to finish, then
go back and work though each exercise in turn, and make sure that you
understand the theory and terminology that each exercise introduces, before
moving on to the next. Resist the temptation to go straight to the stabbing
your mates in the face exercises: if you lay the foundations correctly, then
said stabbing is both more effective to do, and easier for you to avoid.

The photographs are guides to realising the text; bear in mind that the
pictures represent an individual's unique way of executing the given drill. If
in doubt, follow the written instructions. Every photograph gives an example
that I consider to be within the bounds of correct technique; but every body
is different, and there are quite large variations in how any particluar
position is shown throughout this book. For the "perfect" form, please refer
to Capo Ferro's original plates!

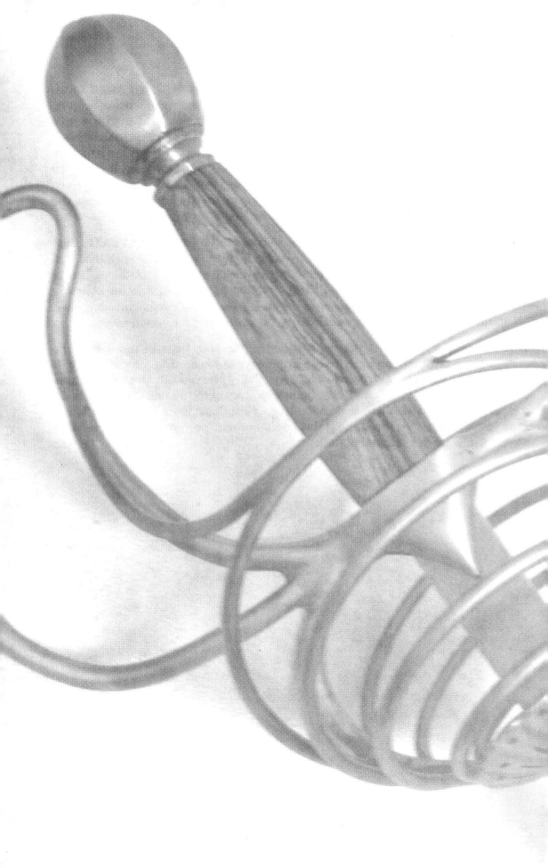

Chapter 1

The Weapon

Capo Ferro refers to the weapon he is writing about as simply "spada", a sword. It is certainly a rapier as most people understand the term: the Oxford English Dictionary has it as: "a light, slender sword used for thrusting".

The term "rapier" is very imprecise, covering a range of hilt styles, blade lengths, etc. It has been variously used to describe everything from a bronze-age thrusting sword (in archaeological texts) to a sports sabre with a funny grip (in a modern SCA equipment catalogue). The word is probably not Italian at all; according to the OED it comes from a German, Dutch or possibly French root. Meyer for example refers to the "rappier".[1] The term as it was used in English sources in the period in question (the late sixteenth and early seventeenth century) describes a complex-hilted sword with a long slim blade, used mainly for thrusting.

A glance at the historical record shows swords we would call rapiers in an abundance of different weights, lengths, hilt configurations, points of balance, etc. For the sake of practicality, I will confine this chapter to the kind of swords that Capo Ferro's method appears to be designed for, and take you though the main classifications that are part of the modern swordsman's jargon. Further reading on this topic should include A.V. Norman's *The Rapier & Small-Sword 1460 to 1820*,[2] and Oakeshott's *European Weapons and Armour, from the Renaissance to the Industrial Revolution*[3].

It may be so that the fundamental principles of swordsmanship found in Capo Ferro's work can be applied to every sword type. However, it is vital to keep in mind the specific morphology of the weapon he was actually using and illustrates. As I see it, the hilt type that you choose matters much less than that the blade length, mass and point of balance be within the following parameters. In my opinion, Capo Ferro's system works best with a sword that weighs between 900 and 1400 g (2.0 – 3.1 lb), with the point of balance between 6 and 15 cm (2.5 – 6 inches) in front of the crossguard, a complex hilt that allows you to put your forefinger over the crossguard safely, and a blade length from crossguard to point of at least 97 cm (38") (for short people), up to a maximum of about 114 cm (45").

Rapiers have traditionally been classified by their hilt type. This can be either a description of the parts (e.g. 3 ring closed port swept hilt), or a name that covers a certain style (e.g. pappenheimer hilt). For the convenience of my readers I will list all the parts of the hilt, and provide examples of common hilt designs.

We start with a simple cross guard, also called the "quillons":

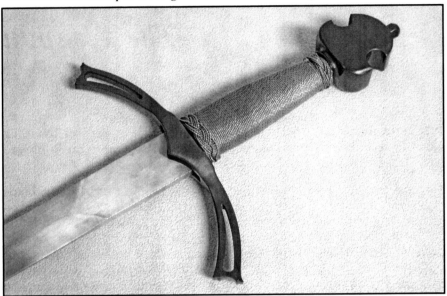

Figure 1   *Simple cross guard*

And add a ring (or two) to protect the finger; these are the "arms".

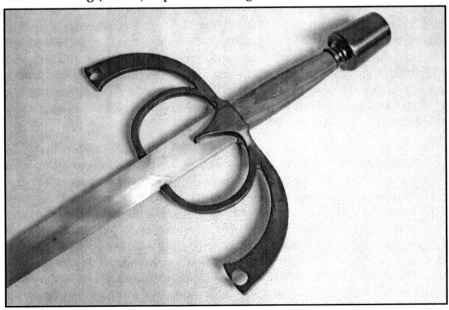

Figure 2   *Cross with arms*

The Arms can be connected by a "side-ring" to further protect the hand. The gap in the ring is the "port", which may be open, as in the first picture, or closed (usually by a pierced plate).

Figure 3   *Cross, arms and side-ring*   **Figure 4**   *Closed port*

A knucklebow may be added, to protect the fingers:

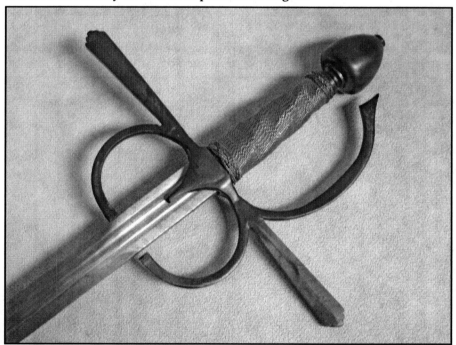

Figure 5   *Cross, arms, knucklebow*

The crossguard can have the forward quillon curved downwards to create a knucklebow:

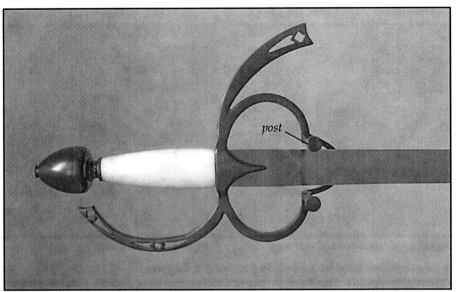

Figure 6 *Quillon bent into a knucklebow*

And as shown in this picture, the sidering may be replaced by "posts", which may be short and straight, as above, or longer and curved, as below:

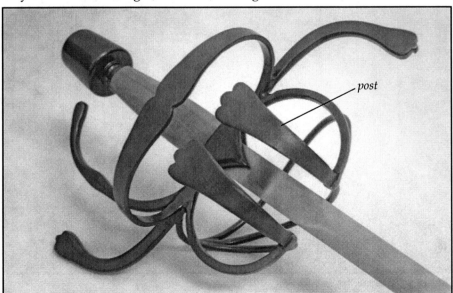

Figure 7 *2 post guard*

A second, larger sidering, or pair of siderings, sometimes called a "loop" is commonly added. This may be attached to the quillons, or to the arms:

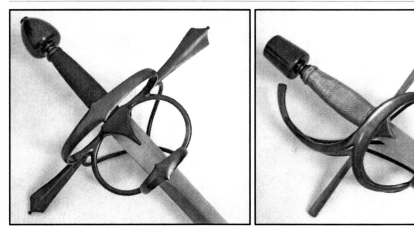

Figure 8 *Second sidering added, to the quillions* **Figure 9** *Loop added to the arms*

From here, any number of loops may be added, connecting the arms to the knucklebow, and forming the "swept" hilt: the possible variations of the open hilt are nearly infinite. Common varieties include the "three ring swept", which is the style most commonly seen in Capo Ferro's illustrations:

Figure 10 *"Three ring swept"*

The "closed port swept":

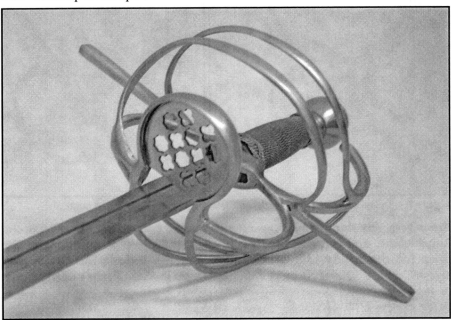

Figure 11   *"Closed port swept"*

It was also common practice to replace some of the rings with shells, hence the "shell hilt":

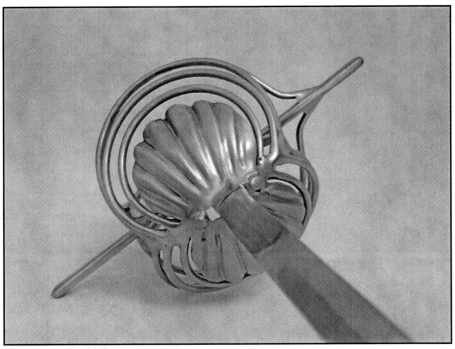

Figure 12   *Shell hilt*

Or to fill in the loops with plates, creating the "pappenheimer" hilt. This is named after "Gottfried Heinrich, Graf zu Pappenheim, one of the most prominent cavalry leaders of the Thirty YearsWar"[4] (Oakeshott, page 162):

Figure 13   *Pappenheimer*

Another common variation had small plates at the port, and a succession of rings protecting the hand, and is known as the ring hilt:

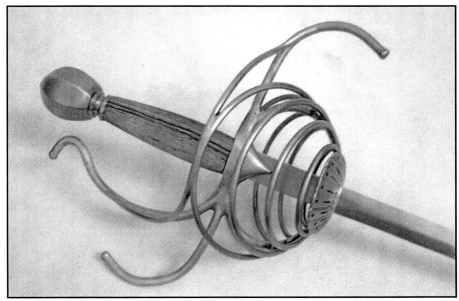

Figure 14   *Ring hilt*

A very practical style of hilt developed in Spain in the 1650s, the "cup hilt". These can be incredibly lavish, with piercing work and carvings, or very plain. The sweeps and curlicues of the swept hilt are replaced with a cup-shaped guard over the quillons:

Figure 15   *Cup hilt*

The so-called "English hilt", according to Oakeshott[5], comes in two main forms: a variation on the three-ring swept hilt, and a strange, saucer-like lower hilt. The more common form is shown here:

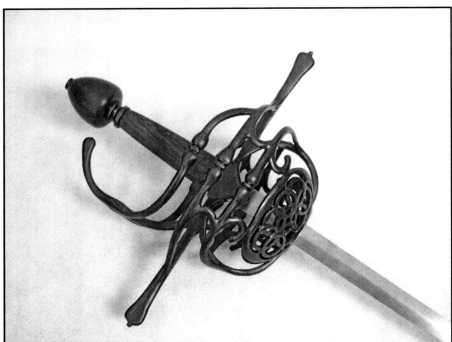

Figure 16   *English rapier*

This overview is by no means comprehensive: there are Bilbo hilts, Cavalier hilts, transitional hilts, dish hilts, loop hilts, and any number of variations on them. However, if you know the names of the parts of the hilt, you can at least accurately describe the hilt in question, even if you can't date it or name it.

The side of the hilt that shows when the sword is hanging in its scabbard, and which will be on the outside when the sword is drawn, is often more complex, and may be more lavishly decorated, than the side that is next to the body. This is primarily for financial reasons: there's no point spending money on decorations no-one will see until you are about to kill them.

In addition to the hilt, the parts of the blade are:

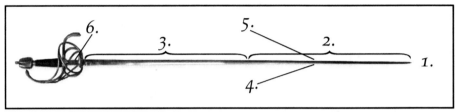

Figure 17   *Parts of the blade*

1. Point: the dangerous end.
2. Debole: the "weak" of the sword, the half of the blade furthest away from its owner.
3. Forte: The "strong" of the sword, the half of the blade closest to its owner.
4. True edge: the edge facing away from the hand.
5. False edge: the edge facing the user.
6. Ricasso: a blunt section of blade by the hilt.

These distinctions are largely applicable to all fencing styles. Different systems may call the false edge the back edge or the short edge, and other masters may divide the blade into three or more sections, but the general idea is the same. These distinctions are vitally important because the parts of the blade all have separate functions. Techniques that work every time with the true edge may fail with the false: likewise, controlling your opponent's weapon almost always depends on you using the forte of your sword against the debole of his, to get a leverage advantage. Incidentally, Capo Ferro (in Table, 39) only divides the debole into true and false edges, and states that the forte doesn't need edges at all because it is only used for parrying.

The Sidesword, and the Smallsword

The rapier was preceded by its beefier forebear, the sidesword, and replaced by it's lighter offspring, the smallsword. For the sake of putting the rapier in its context, I'll briefly discuss them here.

The term "sidesword" is, as far as I can determine, a recent convention, to differentiate between primarily cutting swords from the mid fifteenth to late sixteenth centuries, and the thrust-oriented rapier. The historical treatises dealing with either type just refer to the "spada", or occasionally, in the case of what we now call the sidesword, a "spada da filo", or "edge sword".

Sideswords come in many different forms, of course, but the hilt nomenclature is the same as for a rapier. The figures 3 and 6 above show two of the more common styles.

The smallsword refers to the successor of the rapier, popular from about 1650 to the end of the eighteenth century (and surviving to this day in some civilian ceremonial forms, such as the Finnish PhD regalia). The smallsword was shorter than the rapier, with a blade length of about 33" to 36" (approx. 84 cm to 92 cm), and was lighter, weighing in between 500 and 1000 g (approx. 1 — 2 lb). It would often have a triangular section blade, and usually a relatively simple shell guard, with or without arms. One interesting variation on the smallsword, the colichemarde, had a broad forte, suddenly narrowing at about the middle of the blade.

The following figure, showing the sidesword, the rapier and the smallsword (all from my collection of training weapons), highlights the changes:

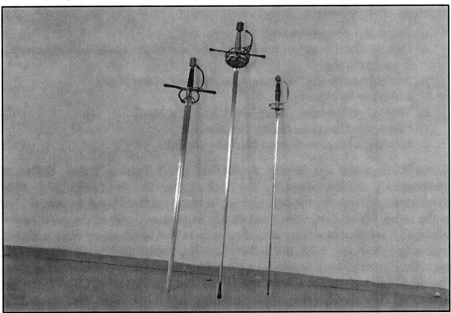

Figure 18   *Sidesword, rapier, smallsword*

Chapter 2

Equipment

It is vital to begin the study of rapier with a weapon that handles as closely as possible to that used in the period. I have often seen historical fencers floundering in their studies because they are using inappropriate weapons. The rapier must be of the correct length. A modern sports epee blade is just not long enough for the plays to make sense.

Capo Ferro specifies the length of your weapon: twice the length of your arm (he doesn't specify where the arm begins or ends), or the same length as your lunge, or from foot to armpit. Unfortunately, while these may all be the same length for him, they are not for me or for any of my students thus measured. My arm is 52 cm, shoulder to wrist; my lunge about 120 cm from heel to heel, and it is about 140 cm from my foot to my armpit when standing. When standing on guard, it is about 115 cm from floor to armpit. When in the lunge, it is about 104 cm from foot to armpit. Also, it is not clear whether he refers to the length of the blade, or of the whole sword.

If we resort to the unreliable practice of measuring the illustrations, in the picture of the lunge, the sword blade is 73 mm, the arm from wrist to armpit 37 mm, and the line G (front heel to front armpit) 55 mm. The distance between the feet is 67 mm.

So, the measurement most consistent with the text would appear to be the length of the arm, from wrist to armpit, as it approximately correlates to half the length of the blade.

Given this as a guide, my blade ought to be 104 cm or about 41″ long from the guard to the point.

There are many manufacturers currently producing training rapiers; the ones I have significant experience with are:

Darkwood Armory:

This is perhaps the best supplier of training rapiers. Scott Wilson can produce almost any rapier design, with the blade any length you want up to 45 inches (114 cm), and all at a very reasonable price.

Arms and Armor:

For historically accurate reproductions, Craig Johnson and Chris Poor are second-to-none. They have recently branched out into training swords, including superb longswords, and a gorgeous rapier that they made for me. As yet the practice blades are not in production, but you can order what you want custom made. Their work is significantly more costly than Darkwood Armory, but you do get what you pay for and then some.

Del Tin:

The premier European supplier of rapiers, all beautiful and worth waiting the standard 10 months for. Their blades are available in the standard 40" (101 cm) length only. I have had several of their blades in constant use in the salle for four years now, and they are still working perfectly.

Leon Paul:

This supplier of sport-fencing equipment has started producing a rapier blade designed by historical rapier exponent Andrew Feest, known as the Feespada. It is available only at 40" (101 cm), and mine was tempered a little too soft for durability, but when fitted to a Darkwood Armory hilt, it handled very closely to the historical originals I have compared it with.

When I first started rapier fencing, there were practically no long blades available, so I made do with sport-blades on theatrical handles. The result was great fun, but a disaster in historical fencing terms; please do not waste your time by trying to do historical rapier with a short blade. There are now plenty of manufacturers in the market, and no excuses!

Whatever blade you choose, ensure that the tip is bated, and covered with a rubber button. Buttons wear through quite fast, so constantly check yours and replace when necessary. If you are using archery blunts to cover a larger blade, I find a .32 revolver shell casing inside the blunt really helps prevent the blade from pushing through, though it can affect the balance a little.

Whether you chose a ring hilt, swept hit, cup hilt or pappenheimer, doesn't really matter. There are a few techniques that are easier with straight quillons, and a few that can be fudged if you have a cup hilt (do it wrong with a swept hilt and you get poked on the fingers), but really it is a matter of taste. A purist might require exact copies of the weapons illustrated in the text, but I have found the method works equally well with my pappenheimer, or my swept hilt.

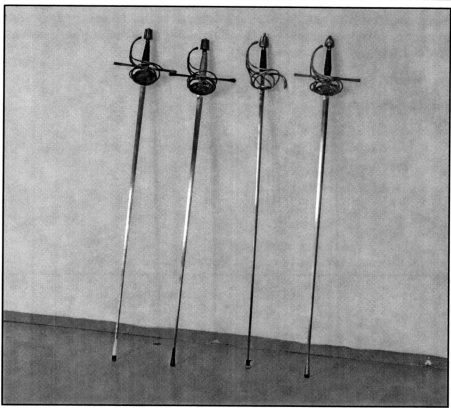

Figure 19 *Training rapiers*

A fencing mask is an absolute requirement when practising with a partner. The majority of rapier attacks are thrusts, and they are usually aimed at the face. The first blow Capo Ferro has us employ is a thrust "to his left eye" (plate 7). Only a mask can adequately protect against such blows, and even then only when the blade is designed to bend, and has a safe rubber tip.

A fencing jacket rated at at least 550 Newtons will protect against the sword actually entering your body, and as such is vital, but will do little to prevent bruising or broken ribs. Jackets are adequate protection against sport foils, epees and sabres, not against the heavier rapier. So your jacket should be covered with a plastron. Fencing coaches' plastrons are OK, though usually a little light. Mine comes from Triplette Competition Arms, and has served me well. Women should always wear breast protectors, even during slow drills.

Rigid throat protection is essential; a point may slip under a mask with ease, and crush your larynx. So you need a metal or leather gorget, with a lip to catch rising points.

Fencing gloves are a very good idea, particularly those with padding all the way to the fingers. The cuffs must extend at least 4" (10 cm) up the arm, and go over the jacket sleeve. This prevents a point slipping up your sleeve, catching in your elbow and wreaking horrible damage.

If you are using cuts, or if there is any likelihood of a bad parry catching your partner on a knee or an elbow, elbow and knee pads are useful. It doesn't take much to really hurt these joints.

So, protective gear in order of purchase:

For slow drill practice:

1. Mask
2. Jacket (and breast protectors for women)
3. Gloves

For fast drills and freeplay:

4. Gorget
5. Plastron
6. Groin protection for men ("cup")
7. Elbow and knee pads (such as for in-line skating).

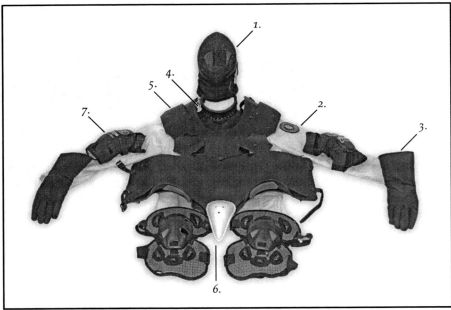

Figure 20 *Protective equipment*

Additional equipment that you may find useful includes:

A full length mirror. This is good for checking your knee alignment, and guard positions. One of the benefits of living so far north is that for much of the year it is dark outside during class, so the salle windows become salle mirrors.

A wall target. I make my own, with a piece of plywood, covered with camping mat foam, and a layer of leather. Additional leather patches to reinforce the target points are a good idea. Wall targets can range in size from a few inches square to 30" by 30". They should be large enough that you are never likely to miss the target altogether; holes in the wall are hard to explain. The main school target has three main striking points, approximately at face, heart and groin height (for a man standing on guard), with two additional points placed like eyes. There is enough space around the target for all footwork actions, for both left and right handers.

Figure 21   *Wall target*

Chapter 3

Basic Techniques and Concepts

Left and right

I have written this book from the perspective of a right hander, and in the knowledge that about 75% of my readers will be right handed. However, all the solo drills can be done left handed by simply transposing the commands left and right. Two left-handers training together can similarly transpose left and right and end up with a technically identical except mirror-imaged version of the standard form.

The pair drills are a little more awkward when done with a left hander working with a right hander and I will give some guidelines, and show cross-handed versions of some of the core exercises. Space considerations prevent me from showing every drill every way.

Conditioning and preparation

17th century Italian rapier is in my opinion the most physically demanding of all historical European weapon styles. This is because it requires a range of movement far in excess of normal daily requirements. Most of my students when starting the rapier have trained with the longsword for a year or more, and are reasonably fit and strong. Without exception, they always find their early rapier training much harder work. It takes no special preparation to enable a student to execute normal longsword actions; but the basic guard and basic steps of this rapier style are hell on the hips, knees and shoulders to begin with.

I have noticed in my school that while nobody gets injured in the salle (long may this continue), beginners occasionally strain their knees through over-enthusiastic footwork with insufficient precision. If not treated properly, this can lead to periods off training.

This can be prevented by proper preparation, and an appreciation of the need to condition the body to withstand the rigours of historical techniques. We live in an age where someone who walks a few miles a day and goes to the gym for a couple of hours three times a week is considered very active. The arts under discussion come from a time when everyone walked or rode almost everywhere, and a normal day would involve more physical activity than most of us manage in a week. Small wonder then that we look at the treatises and are amazed by the extraordinary range of body movement shown in *Gran Simulacro*. How can people be expected to push their knee out over their foot without straining themselves? A common response to this is to decide that Capo Ferro's lunge is "dangerous", and for the body mechanics laid down by those that fought for their lives to be dismissed as "risky".

The inescapable fact is that to practice Renaissance body mechanics, we must first acquire Renaissance levels of general body tone and co-ordination. Otherwise we do risk injury.

Preparation exercises

It is vital that you build up your condition slowly; the body needs time to respond to the new demands made upon it. The function of preparation and conditioning exercises is to stimulate your body to expend resources on particular systems. If a muscle is not used, your body will firstly turn off some of the nervous pathways that stimulate the muscle to contract, and then start to leach muscle tissue away to be used for something else (building up a fine beer gut, for instance). So, the first step to strengthening your muscles is to persuade your nervous system to switch on more neurons to that muscle. This is done by loading the muscle quite heavily, but for short periods at regular intervals.

There is also the question of which muscles to stimulate. Even the most sedentary people, suddenly inspired to begin sword training, have sufficient strength to walk up a flight of stairs: their large leg muscles are in fact plenty strong enough for lunges. What is missing is the co-ordination and strength of the smaller muscle groups that provide support and stability for the joints. So we are not just looking to improve strength, but also to change the ratio of strength. To strengthen a joint, it must be put under stress. This is inherently dangerous, and so must be done carefully.

We will begin with the knee, as it is here that problems most commonly start. The knee is basically a hinge, with about 180 degrees of movement. It is very good at taking strain in the line in which it is supposed to bend, but given the very long levers acting against it, it is understandably weak when twisted. This can be strengthened up to a point, but by simply remembering to bend your knee in line with your foot, you can eliminate most of the potentially damaging twist. So the first exercise is to ensure that you can instruct your knee to bend in the line of your foot.

Knee bends

1. Adopt a wide stance right foot forwards, in front of a mirror or with a friend assisting. Your feet are at right angles, and at least 24" (60 cm) apart. Your back is straight.
2. Push your weight to your back foot, but stay level; your left knee bends, in the line of your left foot.
3. Push your weight forwards onto your right foot, as far as it will comfortably go; observe in the mirror that your right thigh, right knee, right shin and right foot are on exactly the same vertical line.
4. Push your weight back to your left foot.
5. Repeat from step 2, at least 10 times.
6. Repeat with your left foot forwards.

The point of this exercise is to ensure that you can control the line in which your knees bend. There must be no wobble at all. As you push your weight forwards, make sure that you deliberately direct your knee over your foot.

Repeat this exercise as often as possible; any time you pass a mirror, while standing at bus stops, etc.

Figure 22   *GW demonstrates knee bends*

Squats

This staple exercise is excellent for improving leg strength, knee precision, and stability.

1. Begin with feet about shoulder width apart. Make sure that your feet are parallel.
2. Reach your hands out in front of you.
3. Look at the ceiling; this keeps your back straight. (A, D)
4. Slowly sit down, bending your knees. Go only as low as is comfortable. Pay careful attention that your knees are bending in the line of your feet. (B, E)
5. Grab an imaginary handle, and pull yourself up, pushing down through the balls of your feet as you rise. (D, F)
6. repeat from step 2. Start with only 5 careful, slow repetitions.

Build up this exercise until you can do 20 easily before moving on to the next.

Figure 23 *Squats*

Twisting squats

This is my favourite leg training exercise. It is excellent for developing the muscles at the sides of your knees, and for general leg strength, as well as coordination and grace.

1. Begin with feet about shoulder width apart. Make sure that your feet are parallel.
2. Reach your hands up.
3. Look at the ceiling; this keeps your back straight. (A)
4. Slowly turn right, pivoting on the balls of your feet, while lowering your weight by bending your knees. Lower your hands as if picking **something behind you up off the floor. Go only as low as is** comfortable. Pay careful attention that your knees are bending in the **line of your feet. Your back (left) heel can come off the ground. (B, C)**
5. Reach up with your hands, and push yourself back up while turning to the front again. You are now back where you started. (D, E)
6. Repeat from step 4, turning left. 5 careful repetitions are better than 10 wobbly ones. (F, G, H)

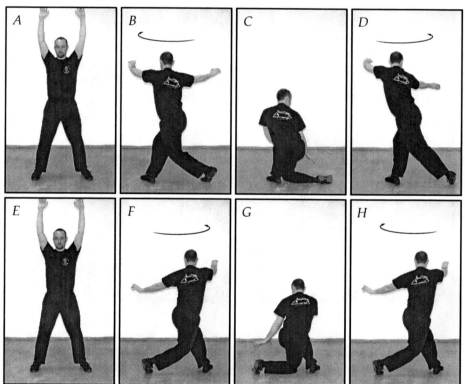

Figure 24 *Twisting squats*

With practice, this exercise can be done smoothly and easily, with one turning motion from each low position. It is very important that you listen to your knees. Any pain in the joint area, stop immediately. Ultimately, you should be able to spiral down to a cross-legged sitting position, and up, and down the other side. When you can do 20 repetitions (10 in each direction) without pain except in the large thigh muscles, your knees should be strong and accurate enough to begin the footwork exercises.

Back bends

One of the requirements of this system is that you can distinguish between bending forwards, bending backwards, and bending sideways, and doing this with either the hips or the waist. Sounds silly, but you'd be amazed how few people can detect and prevent a twist in the back when told to lean in a certain direction. Hence these exercises:

1. Stand with your legs wide and straight, feet parallel. Back straight, arms out at shoulder level. (A)
2. Keeping your back straight, bend forwards from the hips: (B)
3. Return to start position. (C)
4. Leaving your pelvis exactly as it is, bend forwards from the waist, curling your middle back. (D)
5. Return to start position

Hip bend forwards   *Waist bend forwards*

6. Bend to the right sideways, from the hip, so that your arms become vertical, Notice how your pelvis tilts. Hips, shoulders, and arms must remain in the same line as the line between your feet. (E)
7. Return to start position and repeat to the left. (F)
8. Return to start position.

Hip bends sideways

9. Bend to the right, sideways, in the waist only: your pelvis remains absolutely level. Hips, shoulders, and arms must remain in the same line as the line between your feet. (H)
10. Return to start position, and repeat to the left. (I, J, K)

Waist bends sideways

When practising this exercise, ensure that *only* the upper body is moving; there is no change in the legs whatsoever. It is tempting to go further by allowing a twist. The point of this exercise is *not* to stretch, but to learn to distinguish between forwards and sideways bending, and to distinguish between bending in the waist and bending at the hip. These are vital internal skills for this system, so do these exercises slowly and carefully, paying very careful attention to how you are moving, not how far.

Figure 25   *Ilkka Hartikainen demonstrates the back bends exercises*

Guard position exercises

Leaning

The guard position and basic body movements of this system require that you are able to clearly distinguish between pushing your hips forwards (as in the knee bends exercise) and leaning your shoulders forwards. It is also vital that you can feel the difference between leaning in the line of your hips, and bending over your hips. Practice the previous exercise until you can do it cleanly and accurately every time, before moving on to this one.

1. Adopt a wide stance right foot forwards, in front of a mirror or with a friend assisting. Your feet are at right angles, and at least 24" (60 cm) apart. Your back is straight.
2. Push your weight to your back foot, but stay level; your left knee bends, in the line of your left foot.
3. Turn your hips anticlockwise until they are in the same line as the line between your feet (or as close as you can make it). Under no circumstances allow this turn to collapse your front knee; it must remain pointing forwards. (A)
4. Ensure that your shoulders are exactly in line with your hips.
5. Leaving your weight on your left foot, lean your shoulders forwards, as far as they will go. It may help to extend your right arm forwards and your left arm back. Arms, shoulders, hips, and front leg are all on exactly the same line. (B)
6. Leaving your weight on your left foot, lean your shoulders backwards, as far as they will go. Arms, shoulders, hips, and front leg are all on exactly the same line. (C)
7. Repeat from step 5: at least 5 slow, careful repetitions.
8. Repeat on the other side.

When practising this exercise, ensure that *only* the upper body is moving; there is no change in the legs whatsoever.

Figure 26 *Rami Laaksonen demonstrates the leaning exercise*

Leaning and knee bends

Once you can determine clearly which part of you is moving, and in what line, and your knee *always, infallibly* tracks your foot, combine the exercises "leaning" and "knee bends" like so:

1. Adopt a wide stance, right foot forwards. Your feet are at right angles, and at least 24″ (60 cm) apart. Your back is straight. Ensure that your shoulders and hips are in line with your lead thigh.
2. Push your weight to your back foot, but stay level; your left knee bends, in the line of your left foot. (A)
3. Reach forwards with your right hand.
4. Allow that movement to initiate the lean in your shoulders. Allow your head to drop forwards onto your right shoulder. (B)
5. Allow the lean to encourage your weight to shift forwards.
6. Finish with your weight on your front foot, your right shoulder, knee and toes in a vertical line. Your arms, shoulders, hips and right thigh have remained in the same horizontal line throughout. Your left shoulder exactly bisects the line between your feet (Table, 68). (C)
7. Recover in this order: pull your head back, bringing your shoulders back with it; allow this to encourage your right leg to push your weight back to your left leg.
8. Continue the lean back until your head is leaning back towards your left shoulder, and your left shoulder, knee, and foot are in the same vertical line. Bring your right hand back a little, and down.
9. Repeat from step 4. At least 10 slow careful repetitions.
10. Repeat on the other side.

This action is the basis of the body mechanics for Capo Ferro's system; it is **the action done when striking in the narrow measure of the fixed foot** (see chapter 5, page 81; and chapter 6, page 99).

Figure 27 *Rami demonstrates the leaning and knee bends exercise*

Congratulations. If you can accomplish this exercise, you can now stand on guard, shift between guards, and are perhaps ready for the lunge.

Chapter 4

Footwork

The basis of every martial system I have ever encountered is the footwork. Good footwork leads to good fencing. Indeed, every infantry commander judges his troops first on how far and fast they can walk and still be able to fight. The success of the Roman Legions was based primarily on their ability to march in formation, manoeuvre in formation, and stick to formation when hard pressed by their opponents. So in a sense, every martial art is first and foremost a matter of footwork.

This chapter contains all the basic body positions, steps, and movements contained in *Gran Simulacro*. I believe in getting the gross motor skills down first before adding an expensive shiny distraction like a sword. These drills are the foundation of all the actions you will need to be able to do later on, while simultaneously thinking about timing, measure, point control, etc. So afford yourself the pleasure and the luxury of spending many happy hours perfecting your form unarmed, before racing ahead to the flashier stuff.

The guard position

Capo Ferro clearly describes every aspect of the guard position (see in particular Table 67, 72 and 83). Combined with the information in the illustrations (especially Plates 2—6), we may summarise the main points:

1. Stand with your feet about two feet apart
2. with your right foot pointing forwards
3. and your left foot at right angles, pointing to the left.
4. Your heels are in line.
5. Keep your weight mostly on the rear leg,
6. and lean back a little, so your right shoulder is half way between your feet.
7. Your left shoulder is in line with your left foot.
8. Turn your shoulders and hips as much as you can in line with your front foot, so only half of your chest is visible.
9. Extend your right hand forwards at bout nipple height
10. Keeping your elbow slightly bent and relaxed.
11. Bring your left hand to the middle of your chest, as if pushing something forwards with your palm.
12. Tilt your head towards your left shoulder.

Figure 28 *GW demonstrates the basic guard position   Guard position for left handers*

Let us now consider the illustrations. It can be quite challenging to get the maximum information from a static picture, so I'll discuss the guard positions in relation to plates 5 and 6 here. Plate 5 shows Capo Ferro's lunge, but it also includes clear instructions for the position of various body-parts when on guard: the left shoulder, left knee, and left foot are in a single vertical line when viewed from the side, and the position of the right hand and right foot are also defined.

Figure 29 *Plate 5, the lunge (Courtesy of Greenhill Books)*

By removing the person standing in the lunge from the plate, and re-drawing it with the parts in the guard position as defined by the letters and lines, we get:

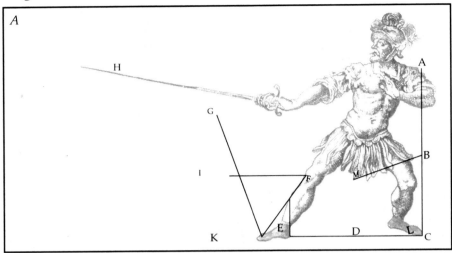

Notice that the figure from plate 6 fits the lines from plate 5 relatively well; the only "impossible" match is G, the position of the right hand. This is perhaps solved by figure D from plate 6, who fits the lines like this (notice that though the figure is flipped, the proportions remain the same).

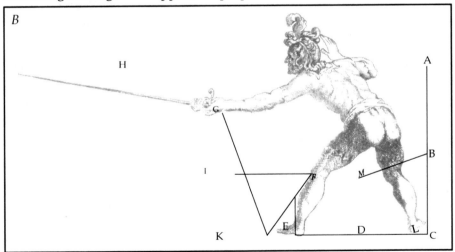

Figure 30

In any case, there are sufficient textual instructions to make the figures almost redundant; and it is a general axiom in historical fencing research that textual instructions written by the Master take precedence over illustrations which are usually drawn by someone else.

Forward guard position

It is sometimes necessary to keep your weight back while getting your sword as far forwards as possible. Capo Ferro relies on this skill in his use of the guard *quarta* and it is sometimes necessary when feinting. It can be seen in various forms in plate 2, fig. D, plate 3 fig. F, plate 6, plate 15, plate 21, and plate 36.

The main points are:

1. Feet wide apart.
2. Right foot points forward.
3. Left foot points to the left.
4. Heels in line.
5. Left knee, and foot in line vertically, weight back.
6. Left knee bends in line with left foot.
7. Lean forward so there is an acute angle between your torso and your right thigh.
8. Head leans a little forwards.
9. Right hand extended forwards with a relaxed elbow.
10. Shoulders in line with hips in line with the line between your feet.
11. Left hand position in the centre of the chest, palm forwards.

Figure 31 *Harri Ahlgren demonstrates the forward guard position*

Incidentally, if you withdraw your right foot, you get a position identical to the usual guard position seen in Fabris' *Scienza*.[1]

Figure 32 *Fabris guard position, plate 14 (courtesy of Tom Leoni)*

Striking: the "lean"

The shift between the normal and the forwards guard positions can become a strike. Thought there is no proper name for this action, it is defined by Capo ferro, and is used in *"la misura stretta di pie fermo"*, "the narrow measure of the fixed foot" (Table 46). Whatever you call it, it is a core element of this system. Referring back to the "leaning" exercise above, and the guard positions, we can convert the basic movement into a strike:

1. Begin in the guard position as defined above. (A)
2. Reach forwards with your right hand. (B)
3. Allow that movement to initiate the lean in your shoulders. (C)
4. Allow the lean to encourage your weight to shift forwards. Allow your head to drop forwards onto your right shoulder. (D)
5. Recover in this order: pull your head back, bringing your shoulders back with it. Allow this to encourage your right leg to push your weight back to your left leg. Withdraw your arm. (E, F)

Figure 33 *Ilkka demonstrates the leaning strike exercise*

You may have found that the back foot pivots somewhat on the ball, as you reach forwards. That's fine, just remember to return it when you recover.

Striking: the lunge

Capo Ferro makes much of *l'incredibile accrefcimento*[2] *della botta lunga*[3] ("the incredible increase of the long blow"), which we call the lunge.

1. Begin in the guard position as defined in the previous drill.
2. Reach forwards with your right hand. (A)
3. Allow that movement to initiate the lean in your shoulders. (B)
4. Allow the lean to encourage your weight to shift forwards. Allow your head to drop forwards onto your right shoulder.
5. As your weight shifts forwards, take a short step with the front foot (about the length of your own foot), and fling your left arm back until it is in line with the shoulders, with your left hand a little higher than your left shoulder. (C)
6. As your weight travels forward during the step, allow your rear foot to turn on the ball, bringing your heel a few inches forwards. This helps you reach further.
7. Arrive on the ball of your front foot with your weight as far forwards as it is going to travel. Your right shoulder, knee and toes are in line verticaly. Your arms, shoulders, hips and right thigh have remained in the same horizontal line throughout. With practice, you can allow your weight to be so far forwards that your front knee is in advance of your toes. (D)
8. Recover in this order: pull your head back, bringing your shoulders back with it; turn your back foot on the ball, replacing your heel. Allow this to encourage your right leg to push your weight back to your left leg. Withdraw your front foot. Withdraw your sword arm. (E, F)

Figure 34   *Harri demonstrates the lunging exercise*

Practice this in front of the mirror, so you can check the alignment of your hands, shoulders, hips, and knees, which must all be in the same vertical line.

A common mistake is to step too far forwards on the lunge, to protect the knee. This is wrong for two reasons. Firstly, Capo Ferro defines quite clearly how far you should step. Changing that changes the system. Secondly, the longer step exposes you for a longer period of time in which you cannot support pressure on the sword; it gives your opponent more time in which to hit you in *contratempo*.[4]

The ability to get out of trouble is essential to cultivate in your training: recovery is every bit as important as extension. Mountaineers have it that there is no successful ascent if there is no successful descent; so with fencers: there is no successful lunge without a successful recovery.

Those readers with sport fencing or classical fencing experience will be accustomed to a totally different lunging mechanic. The best definition of the classical lunge I have come across in print is in Gaugler's *Fencing Everyone*, pp. 11 and 12.[5] In particular, this passage:

> In sequential order, the right arm is extended smoothly, right hand rising to shoulder height, shoulder relaxed, and trunk leaning progressively forward; as the foil arm achieves complete extension, and without interrupting the flow of the movement, the right foot is lifted, toe first, and carried forward, almost grazing or shaving the floor surface as it travels along the line of direction; simultaneously, the left leg is straightened vigorously, knee locking, left foot pressed flat against the ground, and left arm thrown forcefully back to a horizontal position, with the palm of the hand facing up, thumb out, and fingers together; the right foot, as it reaches its destination, lands, heel first (p. 12).

Notice the totally different final position, and in particular the static left foot.

Figure 35 *GW demonstrates the classical guard and lunge with the foil*

It is crucially important for rapier students with a classical fencing background to avoid making the same mistake I did; using the 19th or 20th century body mechanics with the 17th century weapon. Changing how you move changes everything about the system. Be a historical fencer: try to get every detail of every position and movement exactly as presented in the original source!

Unarmed pair exercises for the lean and the lunge

I have developed a couple of simple exercises that you can use to safely condition your body to lunge and lean in the Capo Ferro manner. This relies on you having first trained your knee to bend in the correct line, and being careful not to get competitive at this stage.

Leaning, pair drill

1. Come on guard facing your partner.
2. Adjust the distance so that one of you, when in the lean, can just touch the other's chest.
3. Recover to a normal guard.
4. Touch the backs of your lead hands together.
5. Start pushing your hand forwards
6. **Complete the lean; partner just guides your hand off to the side. (A)**
7. Partner starts extending his hand forward (B)
8. You recover, and repeat the drill (C—A).

Figure 36   *Harri and Ilkka demonstrate the leaning pair drill*

Lunging pair drill

1. Come on guard facing your partner, who is also in guard.
2. Lunge, and adjust the distance so that you, when in the lunge, can just touch your partner's chest.
3. Touch the backs of your lead hands together (you remain in the lunge). (A)
4. Begin your recovery. (B)
5. Partner starts pushing his hand forwards
6. his body follows, as you are recovering.
7. He steps with the front foot, completing his lunge as you complete **your recovery; guide his hand off to the side. (C)**
8. You recover, and repeat the drill.

Figure 37   *Rami and GW demonstrate the lunging pair drill*

With practice these drills should become a fluid, back-and-forth exchange. Be careful not to lean your weight on your partner; if you sense he is leaning on you, remove your support and he should stumble. This is essential negative feedback. Once the drill is flowing nicely, when your legs get tired, switch to the other side and repeat.

Stepping

When adopting this guard position, you will at first find that you can barely move. Indeed, until your joints loosen up and your muscles adapt, you will probably find it inconceivable to fight from this position. Capo Ferro was clearly aware of this; "through lack of practice, tempo is lost for the reason that the body is not yet well loose in its limbs" (Table, 58). In other words, without training, you will be too slow and clumsy to seize opportunities to strike in time. As children of the TV, couch and computer game, we have even more practice to do before becoming truly mobile while remaining truly defensive, as the guard position requires. In addition, Capo Ferro believes that tempo is lost "through shortcoming of nature, by too much slowness of the legs, of the arm, and of the body, which derives either from weakness or from too much bodily weight, as we see to come to men who are either too fat or too thin". (Table, 56). Here I must disagree with the master: there has never been a student in my salle who could not learn to be a useful fencer. Some need more training than others, but everyone can be good at this if they put in the time. And the thin get stronger, and the fat get slimmer.

Fortunately, there is relatively little movement in this system, when applied correctly. You are certainly not expected to go chasing your opponent down a fencing strip while remaining on guard. Quite the reverse; you should be slow and cautious. Capo Ferro notes that the "wide measure requires patience" (Table, 54). If your opponent does not stand firm, but retreats, then let him go! After all, this is the art of defence: "we see that the combatants, almost always resting in the defence, rarely come to the offence, which is the last remedy for saving their life" (Table, 27). In Table, 103 he goes on to say "Offence is a defence in which I seek measure and strike my adversary".

However, it is essential that you are able to carefully and accurately manipulate distance, and the means for doing this is the step. Capo Ferro does not specifically define it, but it is clearly a prerequisite of entering from out of measure into wide measure. The closest thing to a description of it is in Table, 86: "seeking the narrow measure with a little increase of pace".

When stepping, the crucial factor is to minimise the amount of time you spend off-balance, or with one foot off the ground. So your steps must be small and neat, and while stepping there must be no change whatsoever in the guard position.

Stepping forwards

1. Stand on guard.
2. Ensure that your weight is on the balls of your feet, and that you are firmly controlling your centre of gravity. (A)
3. Pick up your front foot slightly and advance it forwards a few inches only, arriving on the ball of your foot. (B)
4. Keeping your weight to the rear, bring your back foot up the same distance as your front foot shifted. (C)

Figure 38 *GW demonstrates stepping forwards*

Stepping backwards

1. Stand on guard.
2. Ensure that your weight is on the balls of your feet, and that you are firmly controlling your centre of gravity. (A)
3. Without moving your weight forwards at all, shift your weighted back foot a few inches back. Be careful to step on the ball. (B)
4. Bring your front foot back the same distance that your back foot moved. (C)

The steps should be neat, clean, brisk and precise.

Figure 39 *GW demonstrates tepping backwards*

Scanso della vita[6]

This term literally means "avoidance of the body". It is perhaps the most extreme of all the physical techniques in this system. The idea is, having set up your opponent to attack on your inside line, you remove yourself entirely to the outside (I will cover inside and outside lines later, for those unfamiliar with the terms), with sufficient violence and momentum to actually gain distance. This action is described on plate 19 as being performed "with a void of the body by stepping with the left leg crossing behind the right".

1. Stand on guard, right foot forwards. Weight is on the balls of your feet. (A)
2. Extend your right arm forwards, in *quarta*. (B)
3. As your arm extends, push yourself around anti-clockwise with your left foot
4. And passing your left foot behind you until it passes your right.
5. Your right foot pivots automatically on the ball, and your right leg straightens.
6. as you throw your left arm around to add speed to the manoeuvre. (C)
7. Recover by stepping away obliquely (off to the right relative to the original line of direction), leaving your right side towards your imaginary opponent. (D, E)

Figure 40   *Ilkka demonstrates the scanso della vita and recovery*

Scanso del pie dritto

The *scanso del pie dritto*,[7] ('avoidance of the right foot') from plate 17, is another means of getting your body from one side of a given line to the other. It is faster than the *scanso della vita* because it covers less ground. However, if you draw a line just outside the right side of your body in your guard position, the *scanso del pie dritto* will move your entire body except for the left foot to the right side of that line.

1. stand on guard (A)
2. begin extending your arm (B)
3. as your hand moves forward, lift your right foot, turn the heel out 90 degrees (anticlockwise) and replace it a few inches forward and to the right
4. your weight immediately shifts to your right foot, and you lean a little back (C)
5. Your left foot turns a little anticlockwise, on the ball, as you move.

Figure 41   *Harri demonstrates the* scanso del pie dritto

Sbasso[8]

Capo Ferro doesn't name this technique, just describes it (plate 14), but as it requires a specific body action, I include it here. Essentially, this technique is a means of vertical avoidance. Just as the *scanso della vita* has you remove yourself laterally from the line of the attack, this technique has you remove yourself by ducking.

As many students find this physically demanding, I have developed a conditioning exercise that will help.

Sbasso Conditioning exercise

It is very important to be able to execute the sbasso quickly and easily without strain. The trick with this technique is to shift your body in the line of your lead thigh: use the proprioceptive skills you have acquired through the back bends exercises to ensure that your shoulders do not come inside your knees. Keep your right shoulder in line with your right knee, and when dropping down, lay your torso on your thigh. This exercise allows you to get the core body movement fluid and easy, before adding in the actions of the hands and feet.

1. Begin on guard
2. Clasp your hands behind your back. (A)
3. keeping your back straight, bending from the hip, drop your right shoulder down and forwards as your weight shifts forward (B)
4. and you rest your shoulder on your knee. (C)
5. recover by pulling your head back the way it came, pushing off with the front leg. (D)
6. repeat immediately, and keep going until you build up a rhythm. (E)

With practice this exercise is not at all strenuous: it should feel like you are pumping with the front leg, and allowing your back to rise and fall easily.

Figure 42 *GW demonstrates the* sbasso *conditioning exercise*

In the play on plate 14 the *sbasso* is done with a step forwards: it is useful to be able to do this both advancing and retiring, so I have included instructions for both in the following drill.

Sbasso drill: part one, forwards

1. Stand on guard (A)
2. Extend your hand, palm down (B)
3. allow that to pull you forwards
4. Step forwards a little with the right foot
5. drop your weight onto your right leg, (C)
6. as your shoulders drop towards your knee. Keep looking forwards, not down. (D)
7. **recover head first, pushing your weight back as your** shoulders come up. (E, F, G)

Figure 43   *Harri demonstrates the* sbasso *drill part one, forwards*

Sbasso drill: part two, reverse

1. Stand on guard (A)
2. Extend your hand, palm down (B)
3. allow that to pull you forwards
4. Step back a little with the left foot (C)
5. which gives you room to drop your weight onto your right leg,
6. as your shoulders drop towards your knee. (D)
7. recover head first, pushing your weight back as your shoulders come up. (E, F)

Notice that even though you retired as you dropped, you still recover backwards.

Figure 44 *Ilkka demonstrates the* sbasso *drill part two, reverse*

Sbasso drill: part three, testing
On plate 14, Capo Ferro shows a relatively conservative duck. However, I think it is useful to be able to fully remove your target area from the line of attack, and so require my students to be able to get so low that your upper body is completely below the level that your hips are at as you stand on guard. The best way to test this, we find, is to hit the offending parts with a stick, like so:

1. Partner stands on guard, wearing a mask.
2. hold a stick, level with the ground, at the level of their hips. (A)
3. partner drops into *sbasso* position
4. swing stick with moderate vigour across the horizontal plane level with where his hips were. (B, C)

Figure 45 *GW assists Rami in the* sbasso *drill part three, testing. Note that Rami is not wearing a mask, as we are doing this slowly for the camera*

If the *sbasso* was successful, the stick passes harmlessly over their head. If not, then your training partner gets a clear indication that he has left bits of himself in a dangerous place.

Once you have the hang of this exercise, let the stick-holder give the time for the *sbasso*: you drop when the stick is coming at you.

You will probably find that your precision goes to hell when you are about to get hit. This is a salutary reminder of just how good your technique has to be before you can possibly rely on it under stress.

There is another way of executing the "bending and lowering of the body", that is shown on plate 11. As it includes a passing step (a step where one leg moves past the other), I have addressed it below, in the drill "Passing forwards, part three".

Passing
Pass back
The forward leg is the potential target area that is closest to the threat. The ability to remove it swiftly from danger is a common component of many swordsmanship systems. In the earliest swordsmanship manual we have, Royal Armouries manuscript 1.33 (a sword and buckler treatise from about 1300, recently published by Chivalry Bookshelf), the author advises that "to attack the lower part will be dangerous to his head",[9] and in *Flos Duellatorum,* an extensive treatise covering everything from wrestling, to swordsmanship, to mounted combat written in 1409, its author Fiore dei Liberi shows a play where the defender slips his leg back to avoid a cut, while striking his attacker on the head.[10] So plate 8, where the defender (D) avoids the attacker (C)'s *rovescio* (a cut from the left) by passing back and either thrusting to the face or cutting the arm, should come as no surprise.

To be able to execute this action effectively, you must be able to move the leg back while keeping the shoulders forward. In practice, the leg going back feels like it is driving the arm forward.

Passing back

1. Stand on guard. Notice that your weight is on the back foot. (A)
2. Start pushing your right hand forward, allowing your shoulders to follow (B)
3. Counterbalance your arm with your right leg, by placing it forcefully behind you. (C)
4. Make sure that your right foot remains in the same line; there should be no turn in the leg at all.

Figure 46 *Harri demonstrates passing back*

Pass forwards

Passing forwards is done in two ways; with a complete switch of alignment from right foot forward to left foot forward, as seen for example on plates 9, 12 and 13, or alternately maintaining the angle of the left foot, as seen on plate 11. As a general rule, you do the former when intending to use your left hand to grab your opponent's sword, and the latter when simply avoiding.

Capo Ferro discusses standing on guard with the left foot forward in Explanations 11, entitled Against the Guard of the Left Foot. He is clearly opposed to it, except in the specific circumstance of facing a left-hander when armed with sword and dagger. So the pass forward in measure is only done as an offensive action. Do not just switch sides.

Passing forwards: part one

1. Stand on guard. Notice that your weight is firmly fixed on the back foot. (A)
2. Start pushing your right hand forward, allowing your shoulders to follow. (B)
3. As your weight travels forwards, allow the right foot to pivot on the ball, (C)
4. reach forwards with your left hand, allowing your shoulders to turn with it,
5. and step forwards with your left foot, pointing it forwards
6. arriving on the ball of the foot
7. and transferring your weight forwards onto your left leg. (D)

Figure 47 *Ilkka demonstrates the passing forwards exercise, part one*

Passing forwards: part two

1. Stand on guard. Notice that your weight is firmly fixed on the back foot. (A)
2. Start pushing your right hand forward, allowing your shoulders to follow. (B)
3. As your weight travels forwards, allow the right foot to pivot on the ball, (C)
4. and step forwards with your left foot,
   maintaining its alignment, i.e. pointing to your left side, (C)
5. and keeping your shoulders turned so the right leads.
6. Arrive on the ball of the foot
7. and transfer your weight forwards onto your left leg.
   Your right hand still leads (D)

Figure 48 *Ilkka demonstrates the passing forwards*

The danger with this second type of pass is that it is much harder to ensure that your left knee bends properly in line with your left foot. It requires a **certain flexibility in the hips, so work up to this slowly, and do not pass** deeply forwards until your joints are ready for it. As always, if you get any **pain in the joints, stop doing this and build up some flexibility, strength and** stability before trying again. Twisting squats are an especially good preparation for this action.

Passing forwards: part three

1. Stand on guard. Notice that your weight is firmly fixedon the back foot. (A)
2. Start pushing your right hand forward, allowing your shoulders to follow. (B)
3. As your weight travels forwards, allow the right foot to pivot on the ball, and your shoulders to lower, (C)
4. and step forwards with your left foot, maintaining its alignment, pointing to your left side,
5. and keeping your shoulders turned so the right leads.
6. Arrive on the ball of the foot
7. and transfer your weight forwards onto your left leg. Your right hand still leads
8. and drop your shoulders down even further. (D)

Figure 49 *Ilkka demonstrates the passing forwards exercise, part three*

By now you should have a fair idea of the range of movement required by this system, and be able to accurately distinguish between s step, a lean, a pass, a lunge, and the types of avoidance actions available to you. When you are able to do all of the above drills and exercises without strain or difficulty, it is time to get to grips with the sword itself.

Chapter 5

Armed Practice:
Solo Drills

This chapter will take you through the basic skills of handling the rapier, from standing on guard, to thrusting, cutting and executing all the footwork actions against targets. Basic solo sword handling is the fundamental skill behind success in fencing. Before you can plot an opponent's downfall effectively, you must become one with the tool you will use. An experienced car driver doesn't think about the pedals or the wheels: he decides where to go, and directs the vehicle automatically. So you should practice solo sword exercises until you no longer need to think about the sword itself at all.

Holding the sword

Capo Ferro does not discuss the grip. The plates indicate, and practice has shown that the sword should be held gently but firmly, with the forefinger over the crossguard, and the forefinger touching the thumb. It is also possible to slip a second finger over the crossguard, though this makes cutting more strenuous for the joints of the sword hand. To begin with, stick with the single finger grip, as shown.

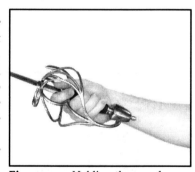

Figure 50 *Holding the sword*

The Four Guards

We begin with the basic guards. These positions are absolutely crucial, as they are frequently referred to throughout *Gran Simulacro*, and many techniques depend on you being in the right one at the right time. He shows six discrete guard positions. However, five and six are specific to sword and dagger play, so at present we will confine ourselves to the basic four. Though Capo Ferro appears to state (in Explanations 2) that the only criterion for naming a guard is the height of the hand, in fact the plates and the plays make it clear that the rotation of the hilt is equally if not more important in defining each position.

Prima

Prima guardia (first guard) is the position that occurs naturally when drawing the sword from it's scabbard:

Figure 51   Prima

Notice that the hilt is above the head, true edge uppermost, and your point is aimed at your opponent's face. You are in a very refused position, weight well back, exactly as you have practised above.

Seconda

On lowering the sword to shoulder height, you have *seconda* (second position).

Figure 52   Seconda

Notice that the sword is not horizontal; the point is slightly higher than the hand, and your true edge is turned out. There should be a slight angle between your arm and your sword. In effect you are creating a wedge that keeps anything on your right side out.

Terza

Continuing the rotation and lowering of the sword, you end up in a central position called *terza* (third), from which you can equally well defend any line (see Table, 78). The edges are vertical, with the false edge above. I describe this position to my students as being like a spider in the middle of its web, ready to eat anything that comes within its orbit from any direction.

Figure 53 Terza

There is a version of *terza* used in specific circumstances (described in the *stringere* section). In this position, your hand is low, as in *terza*, but turned out so that your sword is clearly outside your lead thigh. This quietly but emphatically closes the outside line, without offering your point (as would happen if you shifted to *seconda*). This is sometimes referred to by other researchers (but not by Capo Ferro) as "*terza* outside the knee".

To find this position from *terza*, turn your hand out to the right slightly, and point your sword over to the right a little.

Figure 54
Terza *outside the knee*

Quarta

Quarta is found by continuing the rotation of the sword from *terza* until the true edge points to the left, and the hand is inside (and higher than) your right thigh. **Your true edge is closing off your inside line (so that anything on the left of your sword is unable to hit you).** This is often accompanied by a lean of the shoulders forward (but keeping your weight to the rear and your back reasonably straight). Point the sword a little to the left in this position.

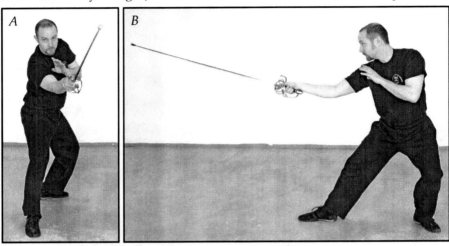

Figure 55   Quarta *held offensively*

Quarta can be taken offensively as shown above, or defensively

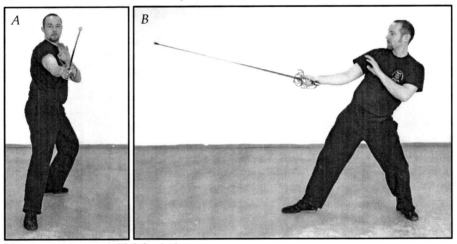

Figure 56   Quarta *held defensively*

It is very important that your wrist remains straight and your blade is in line with your forearm (see Table, 78). Any unnecessary angle creates an opening for your opponent's sword to slip through, and a weakness in the structure supporting your edge, weakening your defence. It also exposes your hand and forearm (see Admonitions 12).

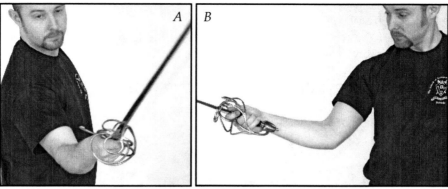

Figure 57 *Close-up of hand and blade in quarta*

Left handers

Left handers should of course reverse all left/right instructions:

Prima *held left handed*   Seconda *held left handed*

Terza *held left handed*   Quarta *held left handed*

Figure 58 *Guards held left handed*

Capo Ferro insists that of the four guards, only *terza* is truly a guard, in that it is the only position in which you should lie in wait (he explains why in Table 98 and 99).

Lunging sword in hand

Though not the first historical master to show the lunge, Capo Ferro does give remarkably clear instructions about the finished position, by means of this plate:

Figure 59   *Plate 5 (courtesy of Greenhill Books)*

Capo Ferro explains the lettering like so:[1]

- *A:* The left shoulder in guard
- *B:* The leg of the left knee in guard
- *C:* The planting of the left foot in guard
- *D:* The ordinary pace in guard
- *E:* The placement of the right foot in guard
- *F:* The thigh and the calf at a slope in guard
- *G:* The hand of the right arm in guard
- *H:* The increase of the right arm, of the same length
- *I:* The increase of the right knee, almost a pace
- *K:* The increase of the pace, a little more than a foot
- *L:* The increase of the left foot with its turn
- *M:* The increase of the left knee of a half pace

What is particularly interesting to note here is that the picture also "demonstrates" (or at least defines) the guard position (see previous chapter).

So, how does one get from the guard position to the lunge position? What moves first, and how?

It is axiomatic in western swordsmanship that the hand is faster than the foot, and therefore moves first. In other words, create a threat before you present a target. As seen in the footwork section, the lunge is done like so:

Lunging

1. The hand moves first, pushing your rapier forwards. (B)
2. Then the body follows, (C)
3. Finally the front foot goes,
4. And your weight pushes forward,
5. While your left foot pivots on the ball, the heel turning forwards,
6. The front foot lands and you are in maximum extension. (D)
7. Recover leading with the head, (E)
8. Pulling your shoulders back out of danger,
9. Pulling yourself back with your back leg[2]
10. Pushing your weight back from the right foot
11. Retiring your foot (F)
12. And bringing your arm back a little. (G)
13. Repeat, but at step one, turn the hand to *seconda*.
14. Repeat, but at step one, turn the hand to *prima*.
15. Repeat, but at step one, turn the hand to *quarta*.

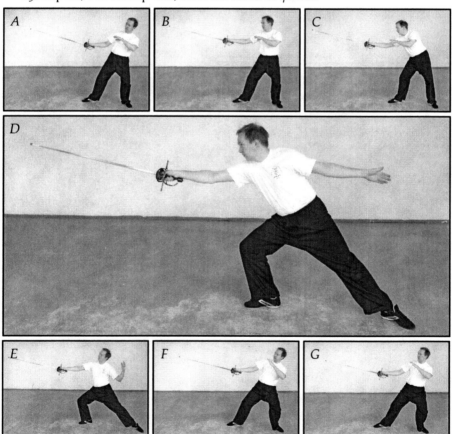

Figure 60   *Topi Mikkola demonstrates the lunge*

All actions, armed

You will find that holding the sword affects how you move. Refer back to the footwork section and repeat all the drills from the lean to the pass forwards, armed. Make sure that *every* action begins with the point of your sword.

Figure 61 *Ilkka demonstrates each passo, armed:*
A: scanso della vita
B: scanso del pie dritto
C: sbasso, *forwards*
D: *pass back*
E: *pass forwards, changing lead*
F: *passing forwards, maintaining alignment*
G: *passing forwards with a sbasso*

3 strikes v wall

It is an essential part of rapier training to learn point control. The ages-old method for practising this vital skill is the wall target. This is perhaps the most important solo practice you can do, as in addition to accuracy, it teaches you distance, power, and control. Make sure before you start that your balde is designed to take the repeated bending, and if you are using a triangular section blade, make sure that the point of the triangle is in the inside of the curve. Symmetrically cross sectioned blades (such as the common lozenge shape) can bend in both directions. Regular practice on the wall makes up about 80 per cent of my own rapier training.

Once you have a fair grasp of the guard positions, and the three main striking actions (the extension, the lean, the lunge), it is time to establish that your point will go where you want it to.

It is very important that when the point touches the wall the blade bends, but there is no "give" anywhere else. Ensure that the blade stays in line with your forearm, and your wrist locks to support the pressure.

Figure 62   *Wrist position when hitting target (GW demonstrates)*

A common mistake is to allow the wrist to "break"

Figure 63   *Wrong wrist position on target*

Or the hilt to lift.

Figure 64   *Hilt lifted on target*

The point of the lunge is to drive the sword through the target. With a practice blade and a wall target, the energy is absorbed by the blade; with a sharp blade and a penetrable target, that energy is used to puncture the target:

The sword/swordsman combination should be perfectly aligned so that no energy "leaks". The lunge is the perfect long attack, with all your weight and energy focussed in one direction, on one point.

Point control exercise 1

1. Establish your guard position, and extend your sword.
2. Approach the target and place your point on the marked spot.
3. Withdraw your arm to the normal guard resting position.
4. Extend in *quarta* and place your point on the spot (or as close as possible). You should be close enough that your blade bends convincingly.
5. Repeat *ad nauseam*.

Figure 65 *Rami demonstrates*

Repeat, adjusting your distance for the lean, and using the lean at step 4.

Figure 66 *Rami demonstrates*

Repeat, adjusting your distance for the lunge, and lunging at step 4.

Figure 67 *Rami demonstrates*

Repeat, extending and striking at all three distances in *seconda*.

Figure 68 *Topi demonstrates*

In Explanations 17 Capo Ferro defines the thrusts as *imbroccata, stoccata,* and *punta riversa*. The *imbroccata* comes from *prima* and descends with the false edge down. It strikes from "the adversary's left shoulder down to his right knee". I interpret this to mean that it's proper targets are on the line between those points.

Figure 69   Imbroccata, *Topi demonstrates*

The *stoccata* comes from *terza*, and strikes "toward his right shoulder".

Figure 70   Stoccata, *Topi demonstrates*

The *punta riversa* "is sent from *quarta*, and goes to strike from outside the enemy's shoulder".

Figure 71 Punta riversa, *Topi demonstrates*

The strike executed in *seconda*, though a common part of this system, is not separately defined.

Figure 72 *Strike in* seconda, *Topi demonstrates*

Notice that the blade is never horizontal; this is because you are always crossing an imaginary sword as you strike the target.

Point control exercise 2

Multiple targets: once you are reasonably successful at the above exercise, it is a good idea to practice striking at different marks, at varying heights, and from all guards. Try numbering the points and have a friend call out numbers randomly; you must strike that number as fast as possible.

Point control exercise 3

Finally, when your point will go reliably within an inch of where you want it when striking in the straight line, practice the exercise using all the footwork actions you know (the *scansi*, the passes, the *sbasso*, etc.). I sometimes execute many steps and passes changing distances constantly, and striking using whatever action is best suited to the distance I happen to find myself.

Point control is the hallmark of a rapier fencer. Practice it whenever possible. I often turn the salle CD player on and off, and change tracks, with my point. When walking with an umbrella, pick spots on the pavement (litter, chewing gum marks etc) and tap them with the point as you go past. No one will notice, and you can get some useful training done while walking to the pub.

Cuts and blows

Cuts and blows are a relatively minor aspect of rapier play. However, half-blows are often used as parries, and cuts to the head, thigh and sword-arm are deemed effective.

The rapier is not well adapted to cleaving blows; the blade is long and narrow, and so has a low cross-sectional mass. This means that at the point of contact, little of the weight of the weapon is available for the cut, and the blade is likely to give a little.[3]

While you may not cut a man's leg entirely off with a rapier, anyone who has gashed themselves on a penknife will know that a sharp edge doesn't need much force to do horrid damage.

However, as the master explains in Table 116, if you are in distance, and raise your hand to cut, your opponent may strike you while you are charging the blow. The thrust is more direct and offers less opportunity for a counter-strike before it is launched.

However, he has us use cuts as parries (e.g. plate 7,), as strikes on the blade preparatory to an attack (e.g. in "Of Some Terms of the Cut"), and as strikes to the head, sword arm, and lead leg (e.g. plates 7, 8, 10, 12, etc.)

I often tell my students "the point of the rapier is the point" (I have a penchant for wordplay, and for repeating myself), but though the cuts are a relatively minor part of the system, they should still be practised diligently.

The cutting action is specified in Explanations 16: "the cuts need to be done as if slicing, because in this manner one comes to strike with all of the debole", and the types and lines of cut are defined in Explanations 15.

Blows from the right are *mandritto*, blows from the left, are *riverso*.

The lines of the cut are these: ordinary, descending diagonally; fendente, descending vertically; tondo, travelling horizontally; false, rising diagonally; montante, rising to the opponent's right shoulder with the true edge.

Falso cuts are divided into dritto and manco, and are rising diagonal cuts from the right and the left respectively, striking with the false edge. Why they are not simply mandritto and riverso as in the other cutting lines I don't know.

Readers familiar with the works of other masters will notice that the names of blows are very similar in most Italian rapier systems; however when using a particular source it is vital to use the terminology exactly as the original author does; so when Capo Ferro writes "strike with a *falso manco*" we know exactly what he is referring to.

The mechanics of the cut are also defined. They may be *stramazzone*, which are made from the wrist "in the manner of a wheel":

Figure 73 *Stramazzone: A-D side view; E-H front view*

Cuts are, however, normally done "with the motion of the elbow":

Figure 74   *Cut from the elbow: A-C side view, D-E front view*

And "when the measure and the tempo support it", in other words when you can lift your arm without being stabbed, "with the upper part of the arm".

Figure 75   *Cut from the shoulder: A-B side view, C-D front view*

The *ridoppio*, literally "redouble" occurs when "with a mezzo mandritto which knocked down the enemy's sword, you will go returning to him another ordinary mandritto" (*Mezzo* means "half"; a half cut is one what stops in the middle of the target).

To recap then, these are the lines of the cuts:

Figure 76 *Lines of the cut (Rami models)*

And the cuts may be made from the wrist (*stramazzone*), from the elbow or the shoulder, and may be redoubled.

The principal use of the cuts as I see it are as strikes on the blades or parries. Capo Ferro devotes half of the paragraph Explanations 15 to explaining how best to use the *falso* cuts as parries, and points out that when parrying with the false edge, use the debole, and when parrying with the true edge, use the forte.

As Viggiani shows,[4] the blows can be easily categorised with a tree-chart:

Figure 77 *Viggiani's tree of blows*

77

The Salute

Capo Ferro does not mention the salute. However, to my mind it is vital as a signal to your partner that you are ready, as a preparation ritual to put yourself in the proper frame of mind, and as a mark or respect for the weapon, the Art, and your partner. The first step of the salute we use at SESH is based on Capo Ferro's plate 1 (page 42) , regarding "Laying the Hand on the Sword"; the rest is my own compilation of movements. Feel free to modify this as you like, to suit your temperament, or that of your group or school.

Salute part one: opening

1. Begin standing, feet at right angles, right foot pointing forwards, holding the sword in your left hand by the ricasso. (A)
2. Offer your right hand forwards, as in Plate 1, and as shown in the photo.
3. Keeping your eyes forward, grip the sword. (B)
4. Draw the sword from an imaginary (or real) scabbard
5. While stepping back with your left foot
6. And arriving in *prima guardia*. (C)
7. Recover your right foot back
8. while bringing the sword to the salute. Blade vertical, crossguard to moustache! (D)
9. Catch the eye of your partner(s).
10. Return your right foot forwards, and place the sword in *terza guardia*. (E)

Figure 78 *Lari Nieminen demonstrates the salute: opening*

At the end of practice, it would make no sense to re-sheath your sword before saluting, so the closing salute is a little different.

Salute part two: closing

1. Make sure you are out of distance.
2. Enter *prima guardia* smartly. (A)
3. Recover your front foot back,
4. While bringing your sword to the salute. (B)
5. Catch the eye of your partner(s).
6. Cut down sharply so the point is down and to the right. (C)
7. Place the sword in your left hand (as in the first position of part one).
8. Return your right hand to your side. (D)

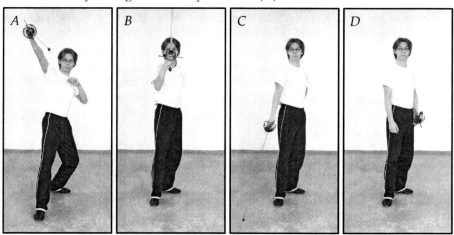

Figure 79 *Lari demonstrates the salute: closing*

Measure and Tempo

You will have noticed that some of these fencing actions are longer others, and no doubt have wondered how that affects their use. It should be obvious that in defence you should always use a shorter action than your opponent; if your opponent lunges, and you must also lunge to defend yourself, you would have to be much faster than him to make it work. So it is useful to have a way of defining the lengths of certain key actions. Capo Ferro confines himself to discussing the different lengths of only three actions: the extension of the sword arm; the strike with the lean; and the lunge. In his terminology, they require respectively a half tempo, a full tempo, and a tempo and a half, to execute.

The term "tempo" is used frequently in *Gran Simulacro* and many other fencing texts, and it can apply to a range of concepts. In essence, a tempo is a movement, or a period of stillness, and a moment in which to strike. Briefly put, if my opponent moves, there is a chance to strike: if he stays still, there is another chance to strike; as I move to strike, there is a tempo in which I may be struck.

This only occurs, of course, when the distance between you and your opponents is such that one or other, or both, are close enough to hit each other in a single action (or tempo).

Imagine you and your opponent are facing each other, a long way apart. He stands still, while you approach. For the sake of clarity, we will assume that you have equal reaches. The longest single attack is actually the pass, but it is rarely, if ever, used as a direct attack, as it is too obvious and slow. So, the instant you step into range for your lunge, either you or your opponent can strike with the lunge. Your last step is in fact a tempo, in which you may be struck.

This last step carries you into what Capo Ferro calls *la misura stretta del piedi accresciuto,* the narrow measure of the increased foot (because with an increase of the front foot, i.e. a step, you can strike). This is, in his system, the first, or longest *misura stretta. Misura stretta* literally means narrow, close or tight measure, and refers to the distances in which you can strike with a single action. This longest *misura stretta* is also known as *misura larga*, or wide measure.[5] (Other rapier systems use the terms differently; normally, wide measure is lunging distance, and narrow measure includes all distances in which you can strike without taking a step. Capo Ferro is unique in calling wide measure the longest of the narrow measures. This is only important when comparing Capo Ferro's method to other systems; just remember that he is using the term *misura stretta* more comprehensively than others.)

Figure 80 *Lari and GW demonstrate the narrow measure of the increased foot*

Now, if you take one more step, you should be able to strike your opponent with just the lean. This is *la misura stretta di pie fermo*, the narrow measure of the fixed foot (because your front foot doesn't move when you strike).

Figure 81 *Lari and GW demonstrate the narrow measure of the fixed foot*

Lastly, if you edge a little closer, you can strike by simply extending your arm; this is *la misura stretta del braccio dritto*, the narrow measure of the right arm.

Figure 82 *Lari and GW demonstrate the narrow measure of the right arm*

It is clear then that the closer you are, the shorter your movement needs to be, so the less time it takes: distance and time are therefore, in fencing, co-dependent on each other. It is worthwhile experiencing this in action:

3 distances drill

1. Approach the wall target carefully from out of measure, and find the distance at which you can strike it with a lunge. A scratch doesn't end a fight, so make sure you are close enough to put your point at least a few inches into it.
2. Once wide measure is established, take a step forwards, and strike with just the lean.
3. then edge forwards until you need only extend the arm to strike.

Capo Ferro goes on to explain (in Table 48, 112 and 113) when and where each action should be used: in essence, your principle attacking action is the lunge: few opponents will let you get any closer before trying to hit you. However, if your opponent lunges at you, he is crossing the distance between you, so you need only strike with the lean. If he comes in more vigorously, you may step back and stab him in the arm. In this case, you are striking in the narrow measure of the right arm: the fact that your feet are moving backwards eliminates them (as it were) from consideration.

Further on in the pair practice section, there is an exercise for drilling these actions and how they are used into you.

Clearly, things will get more complicated once you are dealing with a living, breathing armed opponent. Capo Ferro describes (in Table 106) three main situations in which you will get into fighting distance: when he is still and you move; when you are still and he moves, and when you both move. The term tempo refers to any single movement (however long, and at whatever speed), and any single moment of stillness (however long). It also refers to the opportune moment in which a successful strike may be made. Tempo of course only applies when you are in measure, or entering into measure. Lastly, tempo can be qualified, and used to describe the timing of certain actions relative to an opponent (Capo Ferro defines these terms in Explanations, 3).

Let's say I am standing still, and my opponent approaches. His step that brings him in reach of my lunge is a tempo, in that it is a movement on his part done in measure; it is also a tempo in that it is a moment in which I can strike him, in this case with a lunge.

For the sake of this explanation, I do nothing. If he then stands still, the period in which he is standing still, yet is in range, is another tempo in which I can strike him. So I lunge at him. During my lunge, he must defend himself, and that defence has to happen before my lunge finishes, or he's dead. So my lunge is a movement (i.e. a tempo) and a moment in which he must act (i.e. a tempo). If he has done nothing, I hit him in my first action, hence, in *primo tempo*.

He chooses to strike me by closing the line of my attack, and hits me with a lean as I come forward. By striking me with a shorter tempo (movement) and measure (the distance is narrower because we are both coming forward), he is said to strike in *contratempo* (counter time) (refer to Explanations 3). If he gets rid of my blade and hits me in the same single movement, he may be said to strike in a single tempo, or parry and strike in the same tempo.

He could of course choose to beat my blade aside with a cut (which is a movement, and therefore a tempo), then hit me with a second movement (hence a second tempo). So he defends himself in *dui tempi*; with two tempos, or in double time.

Or he may step back a little and stab me in the arm as I come forward: because this action is so short, it is called a half-tempo, or *mezzo tempo*.

These terms will become clearer when you have progressed to the pair drills, all of which contain examples of at least one of the possible options.

Chapter 6

Armed Practice:
Pair Drills

Opposition

Opposition is simply a matter of keeping the defensive part of your blade between the offensive part of his blade and your body. It is the fundamental defensive principle of all European swordsmanship systems I have encountered, and nowhere is it more important than in rapier fencing. The predominate means by which you strike your opponent while remaining safe is by carefully and accurately opposing your forte to his debole. Most of the pair drills in this book will rely on you getting this part right, so let's spend some time on it here.

The strongest part of your sword is the forte, and more specifically, the true edge at the forte. To give you a clear feeling for this, experiment with the following drill.

1. Stand on guard in *seconda*
2. your partner, places his forefinger against your true edge near the point, and moves your point a few inches aside. (A)
3. Resist his movement to the best of your ability, without changing your position.
4. Your partner repeats the exercise at a point of contact about 4 inches closer to your hilt; resist as before. (B)
5. Your partner repeats this pressure at intervals all the way down to the hilt. (C)
6. You simply observe the difference in your apparent strength as the point of contact changes.
7. Repeat against the false edge
8. Repeat in *quarta*.

Figure 83 *Topi and Harri demonstrate the opposition pressure drill*

It is not enough to know intellectually which part of your sword is most resistant; your body will pick up the concept much faster if you actually feel it.

Unless the laws of physics have been suspended in your part of the universe, you will find that your sword is stronger the closer the point of contact is to your hilt. Likewise, when faced with an opponent's sword, it should now be obvious that to control his weapon you want the point of contact closer to your hilt than it is to his. It is impractical to acquire the very tip of his blade with your hilt; the usually stated ideal point is about 9 inches down his blade (a "palmo"[1] in Capo Ferro's terms).

You should also have discovered that the true edge is stronger than the false, so opposition will normally be acquired with the true edge.

Opposition also requires you to keep your body safely behind your leading edge: Notice that when your sword is out to your right (as in *seconda*), your body is covered from any blade on the right of your sword; should your opponent's sword slip over to your left, you are open. Likewise, in *quarta*, you should be safe from anything over to the left of your sword. The guard positions as defined by Capo Ferro require you to literally hide behind your sword.

Anything to the right of your sword is considered to be on the outside, anything to the left, is on the inside. So when in *seconda* you want your opponent to be on the outside, and when in *quarta* you want him on the inside.

Figure 84 *Outside and inside lines in* seconda *(A) and in* quarta *(B)*

There is a further aspect to opposition that is necessary for this system: I call it the double-cross. In effect, to be safe, you must always cross your blade with your opponent's, and this cross must exist in both the vertical and horizontal planes. In other words, when viewed from the side, a clear cross is seen:

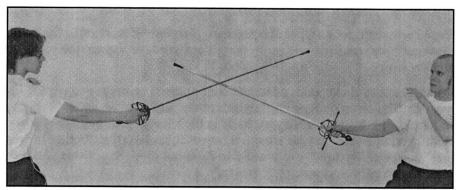

Figure 85 *Cross from the side, vertical plane (Lari and Harri demonstrating)*

And when seen from behind, likewise a clear cross is seen:

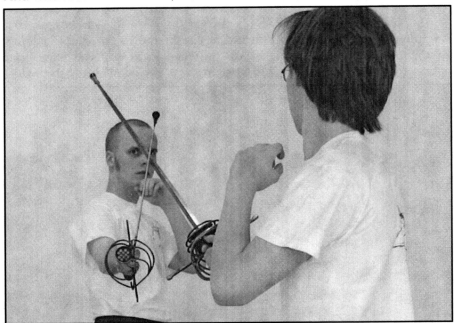

Figure 86   *Cross seen from behind, horizontal plane (Lari and Harri demonstrating)*

The Stringere[2]

The *stringere*[3] is the principle means with which you approach safely into measure, in order to limit the possible approaches and responses of your opponent[4]. Fabris uses the term *il trovare di spada*, "the finding of the sword" (Fabris, 11). *Stringere* is first anglicised in print in 1639, in the treatise Pallas Armata,[5] though the description of the action it denotes there is quite different to that used in the earlier Italian sources.[6]

So, what is this stringering for? Well, you can't just walk up to the chap and stab him; he may stab you back. Instead, you must carefully edge up to him, acquire some kind of positional advantage, and reduce his possible options to a few that you can reasonably predict.

Capo Ferro defines two types of stringering (on plate 6): stringering the body, to acquire the measure; and stringering the sword, to acquire the measure and the tempo.

Which you may do depends on what your opponent presents you with. If his weapon "lies on an oblique line" (which I interpret to mean across his body, so for example in *quarta* with your hand to the left and your point over to the right), you must stringer his sword. If however his sword is "in the straight line" (i.e. pointing directly forwards), or he is not properly covering himself with his sword, you can stringer the body.

My interpretation of the stringering is principally drawn from Table 110, Explanations 12, plate 6 and plate 15. The main points are:

- Acquire opposition with the forte of your sword against the debole of your opponent's
- With the blades not touching
- and the cross occuring about 9 inches up from his point.[7]
- When stringering on the inside, use *quarta*, and point your sword to his right shoulder
- When stringering on the outside, use *terza* or *seconda,* and point your sword to his left shoulder.

When closing to stringer, you will usually find his debole with your debole first, then make the stringering with your forte in a second step.

Regarding point 2, it has been long established that the stringering is done ideally without blade contact; as it is so far removed from most modern fencers' experience and inclinations, I'll address the point in more detail. It is natural for those of us with a background in smallsword or later systems such as foil or epee to feel insecure if we have not established an engagement (a deliberate investigative contact between the two blades). However, Capo Ferro is explicit on this point, in Table 110. He states we are to make contact with the opponent's sword "only in striking", or at the moment of attack.

This is supported by Fabris, who is (as usual!) also very explicit: "It is important to remember that, as you find the opponent's sword, you should never touch his blade with yours". (Leoni, 16)[8] Giganti, on the other hand, states that when stringering on the inside, you should avoid contact, but on the outside you should make light contact.[9]

I believe that this lack of contact is intended to deny your opponent a clear tactile warning of your approach. The eye is easy to deceive, and slow to respond (ask any conjurer): by avoiding contact you can sometimes creep up so close to your opponent that he is unable to defend himself.

It is also common practice to point your sword at your opponent's face when approaching. Capo Ferro (and others) have you point it at a shoulder, instead. Why? Practical experiment shows that by following this instruction, we acquire a better opposition; the opponent's sword is "covered" in a way that it is not when our point does not angle across him; refer to the double cross exercise above to find exactly how this works.

So, you have stringered; so what? The function of this action is twofold; firstly to get into range without being hit; the second to create a "tempo", an opportunity to strike. Once you have successfully stringered, or as you are in the process of stringering, your opponent perceives that he is in a disadvantageous position. Your forte is between his sword and your body (this does not necessarily mean that he can't hit you through your sword, but it does mean that your defence if he tries it is extremely easy). Your point is threatening his body, and you are close enough to strike in one tempo or a tempo and a half. This means that he cannot hit you without first executing a cavazione[10] (moving his blade to the other side of yours), pushing through your opposition, or angulating wildly around your sword.

Stringering drills

The first two stringering drills come, as they should, directly from the *Gran Simulacro*, plate 6.

Stringering the sword in the oblique line

1. Partner stands on guard in *quarta*, out of measure. His point is aimed towards your left shoulder, his hilt is over towards his left side. Your sword is in *terza*. (A)
2. Approach cautiously, keeping your true edge towards his blade. (B)
3. pointing your sword at his face.

Figure 87 *Topi (right) stringers Ilkka (left) in the oblique line*

Notice that in this position you have crossed his sword automatically, because of the way he was lying in guard. I have changed the original set-up because it includes a disengage which I haven't told you how to do yet. When you are familiar with that action, return to this drill and repeat like so:

1. Partner stands on guard in *quarta*, out of measure. His point is aimed towards your left shoulder, his hilt is over towards his left side. Your sword is in *terza* outside his (on the left of his sword). (A)
2. Disengage underneath, (B)
3. while stepping in carefully,
4. and turning your hand to *quarta*, pointing your sword at his face. (C)

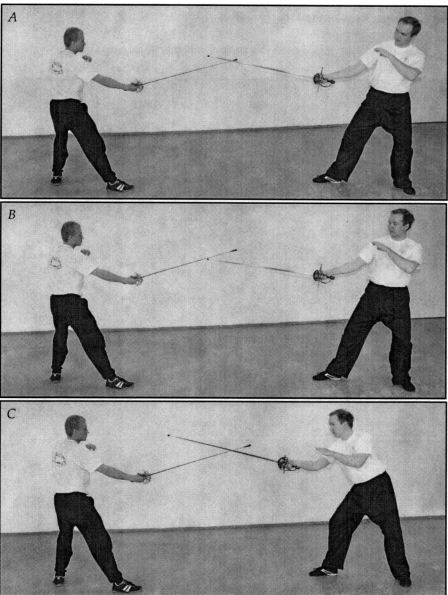

Figure 88 *Stringering the oblique line including the cavazione. Topi (on right) starts with his blade on the far side of Ilkka's (A); after the disengage his blade is on this side (C).*

The text also describes the stringering in the straight line, which I interpret to mean that your adversary's sword is pointing directly at you.

Stringering the body: in the straight line

Partner stands on guard in *terza*, out of measure. His point is aimed directly at you. Your sword is in *terza* outside his (on the left of his sword).

1. Disengage underneath, (A—B)
2. while stepping in,
3. and turning your hand to *quarta*, pointing your sword at his right shoulder. (B)

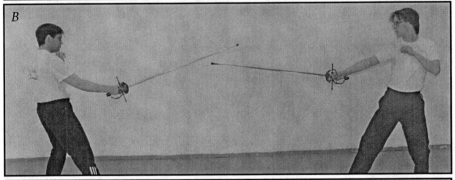

Figure 89 *Stringering the body in the straight line: Lari (on right) starts with his blade on this side of Markku Rontu's; after the disengage, he is on the far side.*

Notice that in this position you have only crossed his sword in the horizontal plane, but you have acquired opposition.

It is also a useful exercise to practise stringering the sword and the body from both inside and outside, starting from out of measure.

Stringering the sword: part one: to the inside

1. Partner stands on guard in *terza*, out of measure.
2. Approach cautiously in *terza*, to the inside (his left, your right); (A)
3. when in the extreme edge of wide measure, lean into *quarta*, threatening his right shoulder with your point, firmly acquiring the double-cross, with your point clearly higher than your hilt, and your forte opposing his debole. The swords do not touch. (B)
4. Make sure that the crossing point is about 9 inches up from his point, and about 20 inches up from yours.
5. Check that you are crossing in both planes; vertical and horizontal.

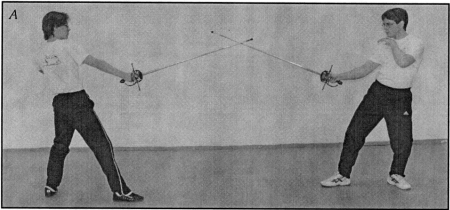

Figure 90 *Stringering the sword, to the inside. Markku (right) has his blade on the far side of Lari's.*

It is also necessary to be able to stringer on the outside of your opponent's sword, instructions for which come from plate 15.

Stringering the sword: part two: to the outside

1. Partner stands on guard in *terza*, out of measure.
2. Approach cautiously in *terza*, to the outside (his right, your left); (A)
3. when in the extreme edge of wide measure, turn your sword to out somewhat, so that your hand is outside your lead thigh.[11] Threaten his left shoulder with your point, firmly acquiring the double-cross, with your point clearly higher than your hilt, and your forte opposing his debole. The swords do not touch. (B—C)
4. Make sure that the crossing point is about 9 inches up from his point, and about 20 inches up from yours.
5. Check that you are crossing in both planes; vertical and horizontal.

Figure 91 *Stringering the sword, to the outside. Markku's (right) blade is on this side of Lari's.*

94

Stringering the body: part one: to the inside

1. Partner stands on guard in *terza*, out of measure, with his point in line.
2. Approach cautiously in *terza*, to the inside (his left, your right); (A)
3. when in the extreme edge of wide measure, lean into *quarta*, threatening his right shoulder with your point, and your forte opposing his debole. The swords do not touch. (B—C)
4. Make sure that the crossing point is about 9 inches up from his point, and about 20 inches up from yours.
5. Check that you are crossing his sword vertically, and that your guard position closes your inside line.

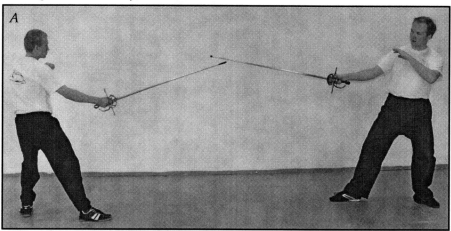

Figure 92 *Topi (right) stringers Ilkka's body, to the inside*

Stringering the body: part two: to the outside

1. Partner stands on guard in *terza*, out of measure, with his point in line.
2. Approach cautiously in *terza*, to the outside (his right, your left); (A)
3. when in the extreme edge of wide measure, turn your sword to out somewhat, so that your hand is outside your lead thigh. Threaten his left shoulder with your point, and your forte opposing his debole. The swords do not touch. (B—C)
4. Make sure that the crossing point is about 9 inches up from his point, and about 20 inches up from yours.
5. Check that you are crossing his sword vertically.

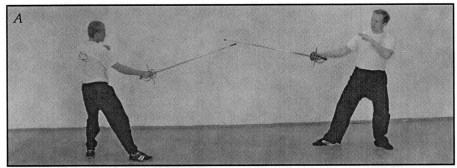

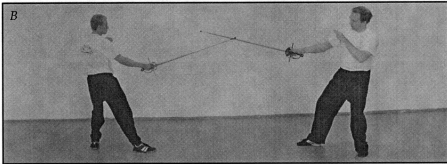

Figure 93 *Topi (right) stringers Ilkka's body to the outside*

Notice that while all stringering is done here without touching your opponent's sword, you do not have to be too elaborately careful to prevent that happening. If he moves, if you overshoot a little, the blades may make contact. This is only a bad thing in my opinion in that it gives your adversary a clear signal, and an opportunity to act on your blade without a prior movement. Capo Ferro at no point discusses *why* you should not touch his blade, but it is a consistent thread through Italian fencing manuals of this period.

The purpose of the stringering is to be able to hit without being hit; so how then, should the hit itself be done? In the very beginning of the practical plays, Capo Ferro introduces the concept of "striking according to the point that the enemy shall give": The height of your opponent's point determines the height of yours, as you must always maintain opposition when entering, or you will get stabbed. If your opponent's sword is high, yours must be also:

Figure 94   *Antti Kuparinen (left) strikes Topi according to the point, high*

If lower, so is yours:

Figure 95   *Antti (left) strikes Topi according to the point, low*

This is yet another example of the importance of maintaining opposition, and an important aspect of opposition.

The three *misure*

Now that you are able to enter into distance without being immediately stabbed, here is an exercise to help you practice the three *"misure"*:

Wide measure

1. Partner stands on guard in *terza*.
2. Enter into wide measure, stringering your partner on the inside as above. (A)
3. Fully extend and lunge. Hit the chest. (B)
4. Recover, maintaining opposition.

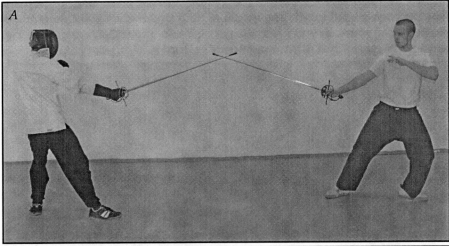

Figure 96   *Antti (right) demonstrates striking in wide measure, on Ilkka*

Pay careful attention to your distance: too close and you don't need to lunge: too far away and you can't reach. During your attack, it is only necessary that you stringer the debole of your partner's sword in a straight line, with the forte of yours, a without touching. When you strike, hit his debole with your forte (liberally paraphrased from Table, 110).

In other words, you simply maintain opposition, without making contact with his blade as you stringer, and make contact with your forte to his debole, displacing his point while you are attacking. If his point is really threatening you, your forte will displace it as you enter, provided you maintain opposition. The lunge takes a tempo and a half to execute.

Narrow measure of the fixed foot

1. Partner stands on guard in *terza*.
2. Enter into wide measure, stringering your partner on the inside as above.
3. Close in a little to the narrow measure of the fixed foot as you stringer (A), extend your arm, and lean in to strike. (B)
4. Recover, maintaining opposition.

Figure 97   *Antti demonstrates striking in the narrow measure of the fixed foot, on Ilkka*

Be very careful to maintain opposition from the moment you are in wide measure, through to the moment you strike, and as you recover. This strike takes one tempo to execute. It seems a little artificial to set up a strike at this distance: Capo Ferro explains that a strike at this measure normally occurs when either you are late, or your opponent attacks furiously, and the wide measure is crossed before you can act (Table 112).

Narrowest measure

1. Stand on guard in *terza*.
2. Partner enters into wide measure, stringering your sword on the inside as above. (A)
3. Partner fully extends and lunges.
4. As he does so, step back a little (as in the stepping back exercise) and thrust to his (well-padded) forearm. In practice you may find it easier to step back diagonally away from the incoming sword. Just make sure that you are out of his wide measure. (B)

Figure 98 *Antti strikes in the narrow measure of the right arm as Ilkka lunges*

Notes on distance

One of the most difficult aspects of this system to adequately practice is proper measure. It is clear from the text and the illustrations that in most cases you will end up running your sword through your opponent so that about a foot extends through the back of his body or head. In many cases, when your opponent lunges at you, you will actually move *into* his attack.

The reason for this is to avoid the last of the "tempos one knows to strike [in]": "when a blow will have travelled past your body, that is a tempo to follow it with a response" (Admonitions, 5). In other words, when striking, if you miss you are likely to get hit; by entering so close, you make it harder **for the opponent to hit you, as he has to first withdraw his arm. Another point** to bear in mind is that a thrust is rarely immediately fatal. By passing your sword so far through your opponent you make it harder for him to strike you back while your sword is stuck.[12] Capo Ferro often has you grasp your opponent's sword hilt or hand with your left hand as you close, presumably to further defend against his strike arriving after you have hit him.

We get around this problem in my salle by training a given drill in three ways. Firstly, we maintain a careful distance so that when striking we do not hit too hard. A full, in depth strike to the mask-protected face can do serious damage to the neck.

A

Then, we deliberately miss, so the point goes sailing past the head or body, as we enter into the "real" distance.

Then, we allow the feet to come to the real distance, but break the attack in the arm (this requires a sensitive handling of the sword; you must be able to feel how much resistance the target is giving, and allow your arm to give once a few pounds of pressure is applied. You arm in effect learns a kind of clutch control, like a torque wrench. It is often a good idea to practice a given drill in these three ways consecutively.

Figure 99 *Markku (right) practices 3 ways of striking on Rami*

One of the hardest part of training an archaic system such as rapier fencing is "keeping it real"; we do not ever expect to use this art in earnest, but to be faithful to our sources, and to enter into the proper spirit of martial arts practice, we must nevertheless train as if our lives truly might depend on our art. The idea behind the above distance drills is this: should the fight ever become real (God forbid; run or call the cops first!), then your desire to live will hopefully override your safe practice and you will have all the elements of a lethal, safe counter-strike trained in. Pray you never have to use them.

The Cavazione[13], and striking according to the point

The *cavazione*, literally, the "getting off", or "withdrawing" (go to a modern Italian dentist and pray he doesn't have to "*cavare un dente*": pull out a tooth") is generally translated as "disengage"; the terms in modern classical fencing are interchangeable.[14] It refers to taking your sword from one side of the opponent's blade to the other by circling your point underneath. Capo Ferro uses the term to refer also to what modern fencers call the cut-over: changing sides by bringing your point up over your opponent's, and down to the other side (Explanations, 14). To distinguish between them I will use the modern English terms; this does not mean that they are done exactly the same as in modern fencing.

Disengagement drill

1. Stand on guard in *terza*.
2. Partner enters into wide measure, stringering your sword on the inside.
3. Moving your hand only as much as necessary, pass your point carefully under his sword, in a small anti-clockwise circle, until it meets his sword on the other side. Adjust the circle so that your forte now crosses his debole, and check that you have acquired opposition.
4. repeat on the other side; at step 2, partner stringers on the outside, and at step 3 disengage with a clockwise circle.

A to D shows the disengage done from inside to outside:

A

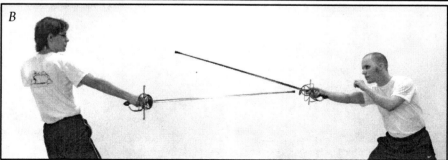

B

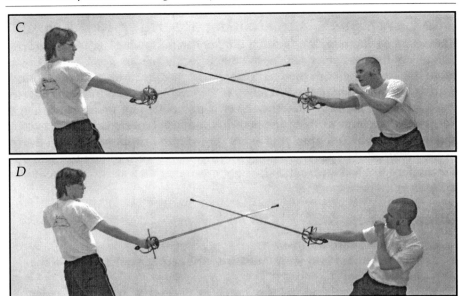

And E to G, from outside to inside:

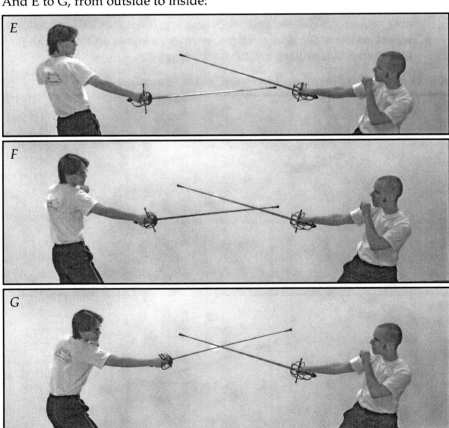

Figure 100 *Lari (left) demonstrates the disengagement with Harri*

The hand should move as little as possible to accomplish the cavazione; it should appear that only your point moves. Given the weight of a rapier, and it's length, it is usually necessary to allow the wrist to move slightly when executing this action.

There are two possible centres of rotation for a correct cavazione. For many years, I (perhaps influenced by my early foil training) centred the rotation at the crossguard. A to D shows the disengage done this way from outside to inside:

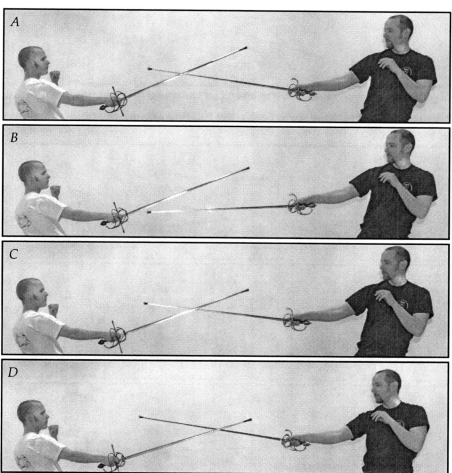

And E to G the disengage from inside to outside.

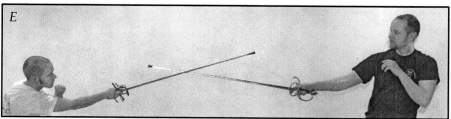

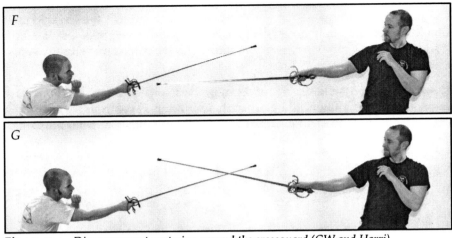

Figure 101 *Disengagement centering around the crossguard (GW and Harri)*

However, it is also possible to centre the rotation around the point of balance of the sword:[15]

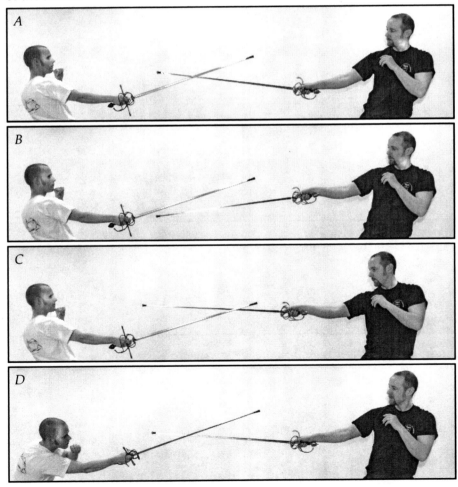

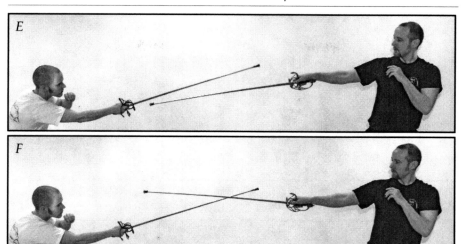

Figure 102 *Disengagement centering around the point of balance (GW and Harri)*

Note that the centre of rotation should not be around the pommel: it creates too large a movement.

Cut-over drill

1. Stand on guard in *terza*.
2. Partner enters into wide measure, stringering your sword on the inside. (A)
3. Keeping your hand in the same place, pick your point up carefully over his blade (B), and replace it sharply on the other side, acquiring opposition. (C)
4. repeat on the other side; at step 2, partner stringers on the outside. (E—F)

A to C shows the cut-over from inside to outside:

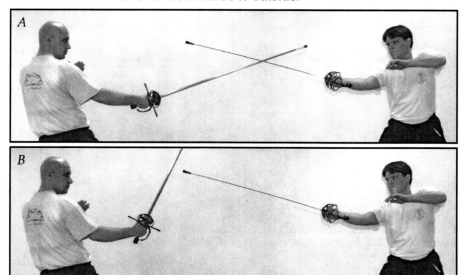

And D to F, from outside to inside.

Figure 103 *Otto Kopra (left) cuts over Janne Högdahl's sword*

I execute this action in the wrist alone; as with the cavazione, try to make the action as small as possible. Remember that every action you make in distance is a tempo in which your opponent, may attack, so every action must be as short and defensive as can be while still achieving its end.

One of the responses to the cavazione is the contra-cavazione, which may in turn be countered by a ricavazione (in modern terminology, a disengage may be countered by a counter-disengage, which may be countered by a re-disengage).

Disengage, counter disengage, re-disengage

1. Stand on guard in *terza*.
2. Partner enters into wide measure,stringering your sword on the inside.
3. Moving your hand only as much as necessary, pass your point carefully under his sword, in a small anti-clockwise circle, until it meets his sword on the other side. Adjust the circle so that your forte now crosses his debole, and check that you have acquired opposition.
4. Partner passes his point in turn under your sword, re-establishing the stringere.
5. Re-disengage, passing your point again under his sword as before.
6. repeat on the other side; at step 2, partner stringers on the outside.

The disengage and cut-over must be done neatly and efficiently, with as little movement of your sword as possible. One of the problems with modern bated and rubber-tipped weapons is that they are far harder to disengage neatly with, because of the added weight at the tip, and the thickness of the rubber. I allow my more experienced students to try the disengages with a sharp rapier (leaving out any thrust, of course!) so that they can get an idea of just how fast and slick it can be.

The above drills give you an idea of what the sword does during the cavazione. However, they are in this system almost invariably accompanied by some kind of footwork action, which will be covered when they occur in the plays.

There are many possible responses to being stringered, such as disengaging and retiring (Table, 111) (this is usually followed immediately by a regaining of measure), disengaging and thrusting (plate 7 et. al.), disengaging and feinting (plate 7 et. al.), disengaging and cutting (plate 8 et. al.), thrusting directly (Admonitions 10) and cutting directly (plate 8). By far the most common response in the plays is to disengage and thrust.

Capo Ferro is very precise when telling you how to attack: oppose the debole of his sword, one *palmo* from the point, with your forte, and if his point is as high as your face, strike him in the face, if his point is threatening at the middle of your body, you can strike in the face or chest.

Striking according to the point drill, part one

1. Stand on guard in *terza*.
2. Partner enters into wide measure, stringering your sword on the inside, with his point threatening your face. (A)
3. Begin the cavazione. (B)
4. As your point rises past his blade, acquire opposition, extend your arm, and allow your body to follow smoothly into a lunge.
5. Ensure that as you go forwards your blade maintains a cross on his.
6. And strike, touching his mask, with your forte touching his blade at the same time. (C)
7. Repeat on the other side: partner stringers on the outside at step 2.

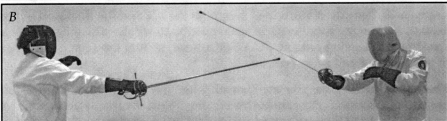

Figure 104 *Janne (left) disengages against Otto's stringering and strikes according to the point, high (on the far side of Otto's sword)*

At every stage of the attack, from the moment your point comes around in the disengage, it should be impossible for him to strike you directly because your sword is in the way.

Striking according to the point drill, part two

1. Stand on guard in *terza*.
2. Partner enters into wide measure, stringering your sword on the inside, with his point threatening your chest. (A)
3. Begin the cavazione. (B)
4. As your point rises past his blade, acquire opposition, extend your arm, and allow your body to follow smoothly into a lunge. (C)
5. Ensure that as you go forwards your blade maintains a cross on his.
6. And strike, touching his chest, with your forte touching his blade at the same time. (D)
7. Notice that because his point is lower, the angle of your attack must change from the previous drill, if you are to maintain opposition. Repeat on the other side: partner stringers on the outside at step 2.

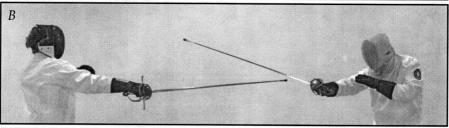

Figure 105   *Janne (left) disengages against Otto's stringering and strikes according to the point, low (on the far side of Otto's sword)*

Capo Ferro provides us with several excellent stringering-counterstringering-attack with cavazione drills in the text supporting plate 15:

Plate 15 drill 1

1. Partner stands on guard in *terza*
2. Approach carefully and stringer him on the outside, in *seconda (A)*
3. and keep coming forwards;
4. Partner disengages; (B)
5. Counter-disengage while he is disengaging (C), and re-establish the stringering. (D)

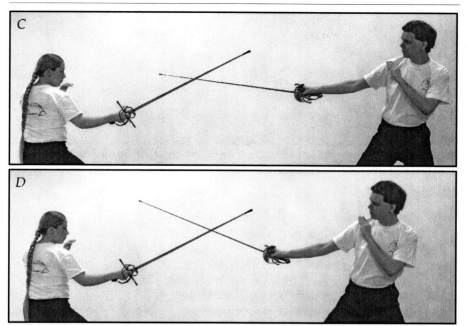

Figure 106 *Maaret Sirkkala (left) is stringered by Tapani Värjölä, disengages, and is counter-stringered, in the plate 15 drill 1. (Tapani's blade starts and finishes on this side)*

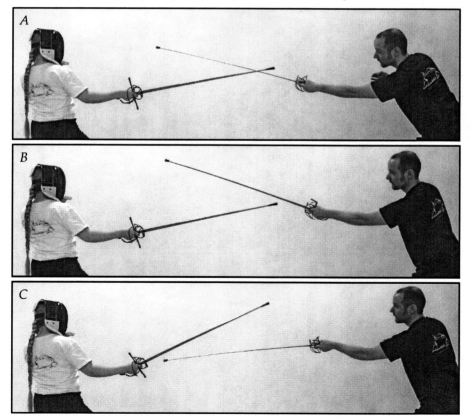

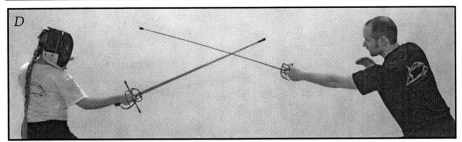

Figure 107 *GW (on right, left handed) stringers and counterstringers Maaret on the outside (in* quarta). *(GW 's blade starts and finishes on this side.)*

Plate 15 drill 2

1. Partner stands on guard in *terza*
2. Approach carefully and stringer him on the outside in *seconda* (A)
3. and keep coming forwards
4. Partner disengages (B)
5. Counter-disengage while he is disengaging (C), and strike (with the lean or lunge as necessary), still in *seconda*. (D)

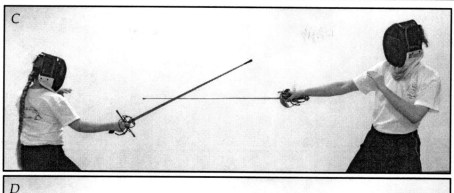

Figure 108 *Tapani (right) stringers Maaret, she disengages, he counter-disengages and strikes, in the plate 15 drill 2. (Tapani's blade starts and finishes on this side.)*

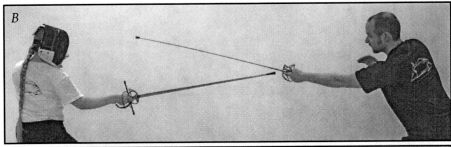

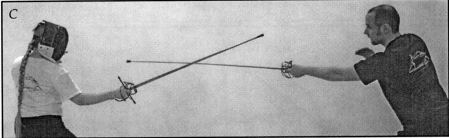

Figure 109 *GW (on right, left handed) stringers Maaret on the outside (in quarta), she disengages, he counterdisengages and strikes. (GW 's blade starts and finishes on this side.)*

Plate 15 drill 3

1. Partner stands on guard in *terza*
2. Approach carefully and stringer him on the inside, in *quarta* (A)
3. and keep coming forwards;
4. Partner disengages, (B)
5. Counter-disengage while he is disengaging (C), and re-establish the stringering. (D)

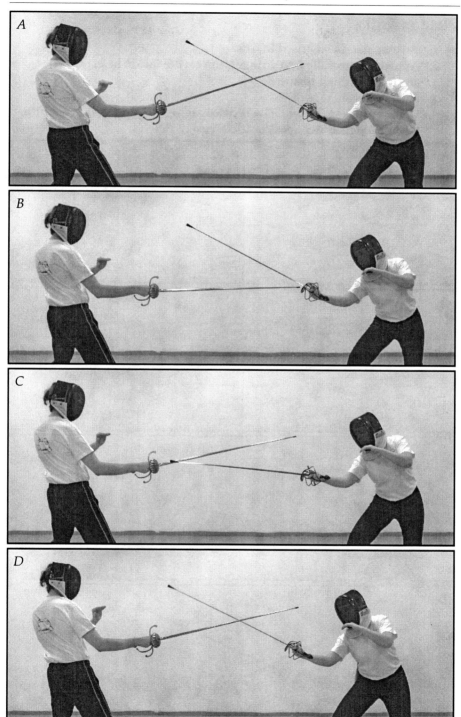

Figure 110 *Plate 15 drill 3: Maaret (right) stringers Tapani on the inside. Tapani disengages, Maaret counter-disengages and re-establishes the stringering. (Her blade starts and finishes on the far side of Tapani's)*

Plate 15 drill 4

1. Partner stands on guard in *terza*
2. Approach carefully and stringer him on the inside in *quarta* (A)
3. and keep coming forwards
4. Partner disengages (B)
5. Counter-disengage while he is disengaging (C), and strike (with the lean or lunge as necessary), still in *quarta*. (D)

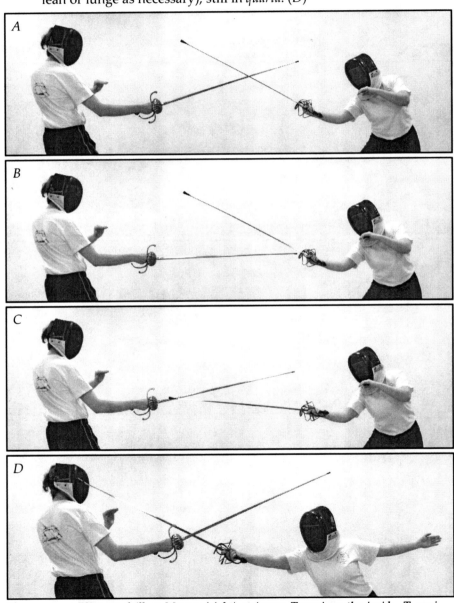

Figure 111 *Plate 15 drill 4: Maaret (right) stringers Tapani on the inside. Tapani disengages, Maaret counter-disengages and strikes. (Her blade starts and finishes on the far side of Tapani's)*

Plate 15 drill 5

1. Stand on guard in *terza* with your sword straight in front of you.
2. Partner approaches carefully and stringers you on the inside in *quarta* (A)
3. as he approaches, disengage, turning your hand to *seconda*
4. with a small step of your front foot,
5. stringering him on the outside (B)
6. and immediately passing forwards with your left foot,
7. Striking him in the chest in *seconda*. (C)

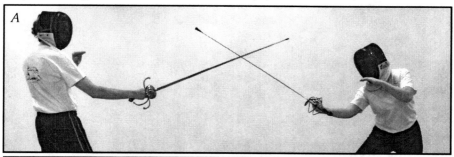

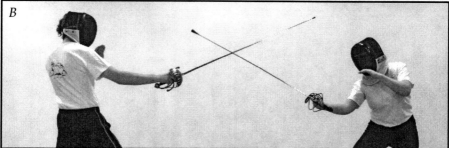

Figure 112 *Plate 15 drill 5: Maaret (right) stringers Tapani, who disengages and strikes with a pass. Tapani's blade begins on this side of Maaret's and finishes on the far side. Note he has deliberately missed, for safety*

Figure 113   *Plate 15 drill 5 (left handed): Maaret (right) stringers GW, who disengages turning the sword to quarta and strikes with a pass. Note he has deliberately missed, for safety*

Plate 15 drill 6

1. Stand on guard in *terza* with your sword straight in front of you.
2. Partner approaches carefully and stringers you on the outside in *seconda*
3. as he approaches, disengage, turning your hand to *quarta* (A)
4. with a small step of your front foot,
5. stringering him on the inside
6. with your left hand forwards near you right,
7. and immediately passing forwards with your left foot,
8. Striking him in the chest in *quarta*. (B)

Figure 114 *Plate 15 drill 6: Tapani (left) has disengaged against Maaret's stringering on the outside, and passes in to strike*

Figure 115 *Plate 15 drill 6: GW (left) has disengaged against Maaret's stringering on the outside, and passes in to strike*

Counter-attack in response to a cavazione attack

The classic play in this system is the counter-attack on the cavazione. It is repeated in various forms on many plates, and is found in its basic form on plate 7 done from the inside, and on plate 16 done from the outside.

In essence, it demonstrates the function of the stringere, the nature of opposition, and the basic theory of timing underpinning this system. It is the one sequence that is repeated in every rapier class I give, regardless of the experience level of the participants.

Plate 7 first play drill

1. Partner stands on guard in *terza*. (A)
2. Enter into wide measure, stringering his sword on the inside (in *quarta*), with your point threatening his face. (B)
3. Partner is threatened by the stringere, and as you make it, disengages, turns his hand to *seconda*, and thrusts as in the striking according to the point drills. (C)
4. As his point approaches, on your outside, turn your hand to *seconda*, and direct your point to his left eye. (D)
5. Ensure that as you counterattack your blade maintains a cross on his.
6. Strike, touching his mask, with your forte controlling his debole. His point passes harmlessly outside your right shoulder.

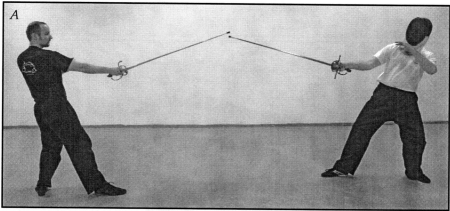

Figure 116 *Plate 7 first play: GW (left) stringers Topi on the inside, and as Topi disengages to strike, GW closes the line with* seconda *and thrusts, aiming at his left eye*

Figure 117 *Plate 7 fist play (left handed): GW (left) stringers Topi on the inside in* seconda; *as Topi disengages the strike, GW closes the line with quarta and thrusts*

In essence, what happens is this. As you stringer, you force your partner to respond. He chooses to identify your movement into the stringere as a tempo, and disengages to acquire opposition, and attacks. This is exactly what you wanted, as you stringered his sword to acquire measure (to get safely into striking distance), and tempo (an opportunity to strike). His attack is that opportunity, and by simply reacquiring opposition, you put aside his attack, and he runs his face onto your point. The secret to success is in how you reacquire opposition. I was at first bemused by the specificity of the injunction on Plate 7 to strike him in his left eye. Surely, a foot of steel through the right eye is equally fatal? I experimented by aiming at either eye alternately, and found that by pointing my sword just a few inches further to the right, my opposition became much, much more effective.

It is a good idea to make certain that you fully grasp the concept of opposition and how to acquire it before proceeding further. To this end, the following drill, based on the above play from plate 7, should help.

Opposition drill

1. Partner extends in *seconda*, threatening your face.
2. Make contact with his sword , pointing your weapon at his left eye, sliding his point offline. (A)
3. Partner moves his point back across towards your left eye, taking your point offline. (B)
4. Notice how the movement of the points causes the point of blade contact to slip, from your forte to his and back again.
5. repeat, slowly and carefully, observing how the blade relationship changes as you bring your point back on line. (C)

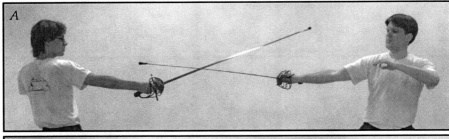

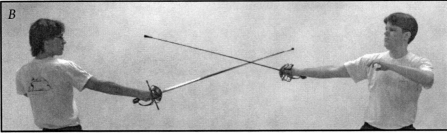

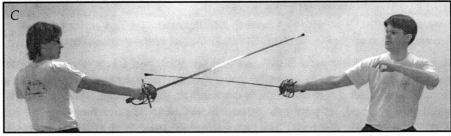

Figure 118 *Janne (right) and Lari demonstrate the opposition drill. Janne's blade remains on this side*

Once you are comfortable with the concept of controlling your partner's sword through controlling the point of blade contact and the direction of your point, apply that knowledge to the other side.

Plate 16 first play

1. Partner stands on guard in *quarta*.
2. Enter into wide measure, stringering his sword on the outside with your hand in *terza* outside the knee, with your point threatening his face. (A)
3. Partner is threatened by the stringere, and as you make it, disengages, turns his hand to *quarta*, and thrusts as in the striking according to the point drills. (B)
4. As his point approaches, on your inside, turn your hand to *quarta*, and direct your point to his face. (C)
5. Ensure that as you counterattack, your blade maintains a cross on his.
6. Strike, touching his mask, with your forte controlling his debole. His point passes harmlessly to your left. (D)

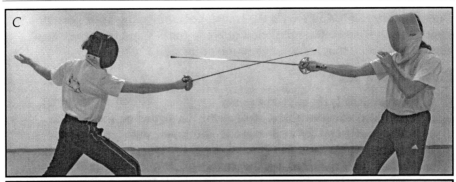

Figure 119 *Plate 16 first play: Petri Wessman (right) stringers Tapani on the outside; Tapani disengages, Petri closes the line with* quarta *and strikes*

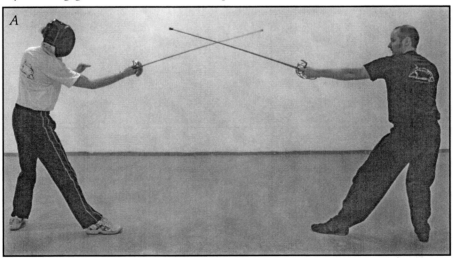

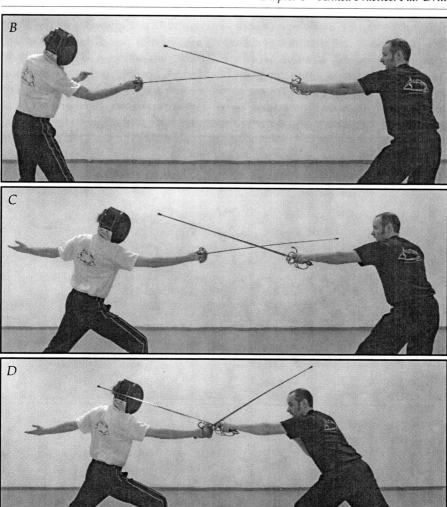

Figure 120 *Plate 16 first play: GW (on right, left handed) stringers Tapani on the outside in quarta; Tapani disengages, GW closes the line with* seconda *and strikes*

Notice that the precise relationship of the weapons, and the feeling of the contact is different from one side to the other. This is because these drills are not mirror images of each other; the weapon stays in your right hand, and the angles therefore change as you change side.

Repeat the above drills, and as the stringerer, manipulate the height of your partner's attack; he must strike according to the point that you give, so stringering high forces him to attack high; stringering with your point lower allows him to attack lower. This kind of control over his actions becomes important when you start to use the avoidance footwork.

Your strike can be made even more effective with a slight step of the front foot (a lunge if the distance requires it) away from the direction you are pointing the sword. In other words, if striking his left eye, step slightly to your left. This keeps you safer from his blade. Capo Ferro doesn't mention this directly, but the plates appear to show such angles in the footwork. Try the above drills with this added twist. For comparison, here are the end positions of the plate 7 drill done without and with that angle to the step:

Figure 121   *A: strike with straight lunge; B: strike with angled lunge*
(GW and Tapani demonstrating)

Contratempo

"Contratempo is when at the very same time that the adversary wants to strike me, I encounter him in shorter tempo and measure" (Explanations 3). In his Admonitions (number 10), Capo Ferro states "in more manners can one strike in contratempo, but I do not approve of other than two" which he describes in detail. Here they are, laid out as drills:

Contratempo drill one A

1. Stand on guard in *quarta*
2. Partner enters into measure to stringer on the inside (A)
3. While his front foot is moving, "push a thrust" i.e. dominate his sword and strike, passing forward with the left foot. (B)

Figure 122 *Contratempo drill one A: Antti (left) stringers Otto on the inside; as Antti's foot is moving, Otto passes and strikes.*

Contratempo drill one B

1. Stand on guard in *quarta*
2. Partner enters into measure to stringer on the inside (A)
3. While his front foot is moving, "push a thrust" i.e. dominate his sword and strike, stepping with the right foot. (B)

Figure 123 *Contratempo drill one B: Antti (left) stringers Otto on the inside; as Antti's foot is moving, Otto lunges and strikes.*

Contratempo drill two

1. Stand on guard in *terza*
2. Partner enters into measure to stringer on the outside (A)
3. While his front foot is moving, "thrust him in *seconda*" i.e. dominate his sword (B) and strike, passing forward with the left foot (C).

Figure 124 *Contratempo drill two: Antti (left) stringers Otto on the outside; as Antti's foot is moving, Otto passes and strikes.*

However, on plate 11, he shows another strike which he defines as being done in contratempo:

Plate 11 drill one

1. Partner stands on guard in *terza*
2. Stand on guard in *terza*
3. Move into "a high transverse *quarta*", pointing your swordat his left shoulder (A)
4. Partner uses this as an opportunity to enter, stringering you on the inside (B)
5. As he enters, turn your hand to *seconda* and strike, passing forwards with the left foot (this is not mentioned in the text, but is clear in the illustration), dropping down under his sword with a *sbasso*. (C, D)

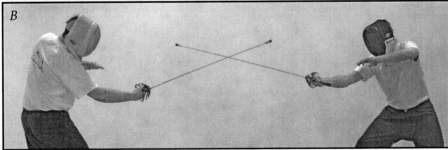

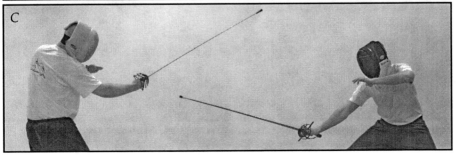

Figure 125 *Plate 11 drill one: Antti (right) is stringered by Otto, and responds by disengaging and attacking with a* sbasso.

Plate 11 drill two

1. Stand on guard in *terza*
2. Partner comes to stringer on the outside (A)
3. Disengage and feint in *quarta* to his face
4. Partner attempts to parry (how is not specified; I do it with a simple shift to *quarta*, as illustrated) (B)
5. As he parries, turn your hand to *seconda* and strike, passing forwards with the left foot, dropping down under his sword with a *sbasso*. (C)

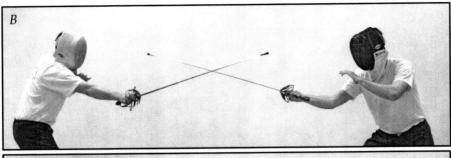

Figure 126 *Plate 11 drill two: Antti (right) is stringered by Otto, disengages with a feint, and deceives Otto's parry with a second disengagement, and strikes with a sbasso.*

Plate 11 drill three

1. Stand on guard in *terza*
2. Partner comes to stringer on the inside (A)
3. Disengage and feint in *terza* to his face (B)
4. Partner attempts to parry "raising his sword"(I interpret this as a false edge strike, a half-cut of *falso manco*) (C)
5. As he parries, turn your hand to *seconda* and strike, passing forwards with the left foot, dropping down under his sword with a *sbasso*. (D)

Figure 127 *Plate 11 drill three: Antti (right) is stringered by Otto, disengages with a feint, and deceives Otto's parry with a second disengagement, and strikes with a* sbasso.

Plate 11 drill four (part one)

1. Partner stands on guard in *terza*
2. Stringer him on the inside, in *quarta* (A)
3. He disengages and attacks in *seconda* to your face (B)
4. As he attacks, turn your hand to *terza* (C) and strike (here the passing forwards is, I think, unnecessary), dropping down under his sword with a *sbasso*. (D)

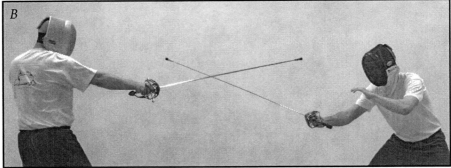

Figure 128 *Plate 11 drill four (part one): Antti (right) stringers Otto on the inside, Otto disengages to strike; Antti disengages underneath and attacks with a sbasso.*

Capo Ferro at this point notes that you could alternatively parry his thrust in *terza* with your point high (effectively the false-edge strike as described above), then turn your hand to seconda and riposte under his arm "as above". However, I do not think that this is supposed to be an example of contratempo, as it clearly takes two tempi to execute.[16] I will include this play in the section on parry-ripostes, so the next drill will appear out of sequence.

Plate 11 drill five

1. Partner stands on guard in *terza*
2. Stringer him on the outside, in *terza* (A)
3. He disengages to stringer you on the inside (B)
4. As he turns his sword, drop your point a little and strike in *terza*, Passing forward with the left foot, entering with a *sbasso*. (C)

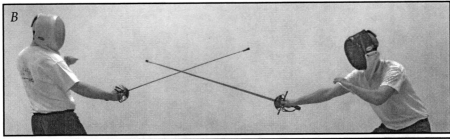

Figure 129 *Plate 11 drill five: Antti (right) stringers Otto on the outside, Otto disengages to stringer; Antti disengages underneath and attacks with a sbasso [note Antti is in seconda, though Capo Ferro specifies terza. (author error)]*

What all these contratempo examples except drill four (part one) seem to have in common is a sense of the pre-emptive strike. Capo Ferro is apparently not using the term contratempo in the same way as it is used in modern fencing (where it usually denotes the time of a defence against a counter-attack); instead, what we see here is the attack on your opponent's preparation, or a deception of his parry. As your opponent tries to dominate your blade with a parry or a stringering, you deceive it or oppose it, and strike. Plate 11 drills 2 and 3 will become easier once you have studied the chapter on parrying, later in this book.

On plate 14, he shows a similar action, in a similar context to drill four, which goes like this:

Plate 14 contratempo drill

1. Partner stands on guard in *terza*
2. Stringer him on the inside, in *quarta* (A)
3. He disengages and attacks in *terza* to your face (B)
4. As he attacks, lower your point, turning your hand to *seconda*, stepping in a little with the right foot while dropping into *sbasso*. (C)

140

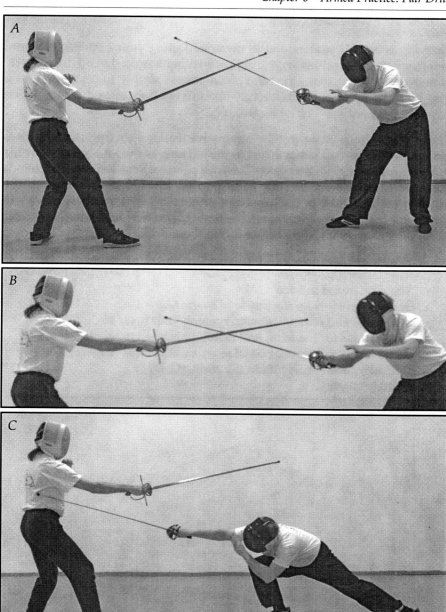

Figure 130 *Plate 14 contratempo drill: Topi (right) stringers Petri on the inside; as Petri disengages to strike, Topi enters with a sbasso.*

The conclusion I draw from this is that a strike in contratempo, in this system, can be done against any movement of your opponent, be it offensive (his attack), defensive (his parry, or his disengaging against your stringering) or investigative (his stringering). Simply, as Capo Ferro states, "encounter him in shorter tempo and measure" (Explanations 3).

Parry-riposte

Parrying is usually understood to mean deflecting your opponent's sword before striking him with a second action. In other words: defend, then attack. However, in this system, the term *parare* means simply to set aside, and it may be done either as an exclusively defensive action, or as the domination of your opponent's sword while striking.

These plays from plate 7 (C's alternative actions to the attack with a cavazione that earned him a thrust in the left eye, as shown above) show the difference. The original text reads *"havrebbe parato di falso, o di vero filo"*, which Swanger translates as "would have parried [the enemy's sword to the outside] with the false or the true edge". Actually executing these plays will give you a feel for the difference in the timing. You may find it useful to refer to the later chapter on feints before trying these drills.

Parrying drill one (plate 7)

1. Stand on guard in *terza*
2. partner stringers on the inside in *quarta* (A)
3. disengage and feint in *seconda*, keeping your body back: (B)
4. partner falls for the feint, and turning his hand to *seconda*, attacks.
5. As he does so, turn your hand to *prima*, collecting his sword on your true edge, and thrust him in the chest. (C, D)
6. retire in *quarta*

Figure 131 *Plate 7 parrying drill one, true edge: Tapani (right) is stringered on the inside by Janne; Tapani disengages with a feint, Janne attacks, Tapani parries with* prima *and strikes.*

Notice how by simply turning your hand to *prima* your true edge forces his sword away (the *parare* part of this drill), and your point effortlessly lines up with his chest.

Parrying drill two (plate 7)

1. Stand on guard in *terza*
2. Partner stringers on the inside in *quarta*
3. disengage and feint in *seconda*, keeping your body back. (A)
4. partner falls for the feint, and turning his hand to *seconda*, attacks.
5. As your partner attacks in *seconda*, turn your hand to *terza* and strike his sword up and out with a *falso manco*, (B)
6. and let your blade drop down in the same line as it went up, creating a natural *mandritto ordinario* to his head. (C)
7. retire in *quarta* (D)

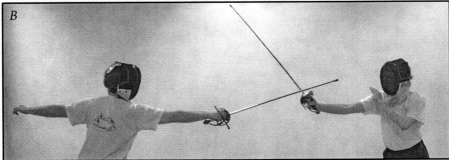

Figure 132 *Plate 7 parrying drill two: false edge: Tapani (right) is stringered on the inside by Janne; Tapani disengages with a feint, Janne attacks, Tapani parries with a* falso manco *and strikes* mandritto ordinario.

There is a clear difference in this second drill between the rising action that you parry with, and the descending action that you strike with. So, the parry-riposte in the first drill is done in a single tempo, and in the second drill in two tempi.

It is clear then that the term "parry" is potentially misleading. In this system it refers to any setting aside of your opponent's sword with your own: it is therefore distinguished by blade contact, not by timing. The parry always occurs before the riposte, but they can happen in one continuous action (a single tempo) or two distinct movements (two tempi). This is counter-intuitive for anyone trained in sports or classical fencing (particularly the French paradigm, as I have been); but we really should not be surprised to find that shortening the weapon by a foot and steadily modifying the system for four hundred years alters the terminology somewhat.

However, we must include the separated parry riposte, due tempi defence, as it is part of this system (albeit less commonly used than the parry riposte in a single tempo). In the absence of a better term, I will continue to use "parry" to signify a purely defensive action, the successful deflection of your opponent's attack immediately preceding your return strike (riposte). Just be aware that this is related to but not synonymous with *parare* as Capo Ferro is using it.

We have already looked at parrying a thrust to your outside line with a *falso*; if the attack comes to the inside, you may parry with a *mezzo mandritto*, using the true edge.

Parrying drill 3 (plate 16)

1. Partner stands on guard in *terza*
2. Stringer him on the outside (A)
3. Partner disengages to thrust on the inside, in *quarta* (B)
4. Execute a clear *mandritto ordinario*, striking sharply down on his blade, turning your hand to *quarta*. (C)
5. Ensure that your point remains offensive; immediately thrust to the mask.

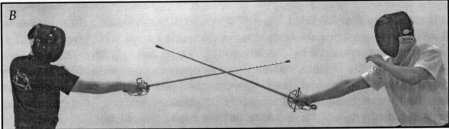

Figure 133 *Parry drill three, inside: Ilkka (right) stringers GW on the outside; GW disengages and attacks; Ilkka parries with a* mezzo mandritto ordinario.

Clearly, the virtue of using a *mezzo mandritto*, instead of a complete one, is that your point remains offensive during the parry. It is surely a bad idea to allow your point to drop out of line during this action, because if your parry is deceived, you will have no chance of saving yourself.

And for the sake of completing the plays of plate 11, here is the drill missed out in the contratempo section:

Plate 11 drill four (part two)

1. Partner stands on guard in *terza*
2. Stringer him on the inside, in *quarta* (A)
3. He disengages and attacks in *seconda* to your face
4. As he attacks, turn your hand to *terza* and execute a sharp false-edge cut to his sword. (B)
5. and drop your point under his arm, turning your hand to *seconda*, and lowering your body with a *sbasso*. (Again, the pass is unnecessary.) (C)

Figure 134 *Plate 11 drill four (part two): Antti (right) stringers Otto on the inside; as Otto disengages and strikes, Antti parries with a* falso manco, *and thrust*

Note the similarity of the parry with the second parrying drill from plate 7, though the prior actions and the riposte itself are quite different.

Body avoidances, *scansi*

The fourth play of plate 11, and the first of plate 14, have already introduced you to the concept of getting out of the way of your opponent's sword as he attacks. The passing back of the front foot (plate 8), the *scanso della vita* (from plate 19) and the *scanso del pie dritto* (from plate 17) are used to absent yourself from the line of your opponent's attack. Do not expect to use these latter two actions against an unexpected strike; these work because you have set up your opponent to attack you in a particular line at a particular time. Refer to the unarmed drills above to get the hang of how your body will move.

Although the *scansi* are illustrated only on plates 17 and 19, they have actually been used in some of the earlier plays, as counters to the actions shown on plates 9, 12, and 18. On plates 9 and 18, Capo Ferro uses the verb *inquartare* (the process of passing the left foot to the right behind you, as in an inquartata) to describe the action (which he has previously dismissed as "worthless" [Table, 92]), and does not refer to the techniques by name; however it would appear that he is using the term here to describe the same action that he elsewhere calls a *scanso*.

Plate 17 *Scanso del pie dritto* drill

1. Partner stands on guard in *terza*
2. Stringer him on the outside (A)
3. Partner disengages to thrust with a lunge on the inside, in *quarta* (B)
4. Turn your hand to *quarta*, aiming at the bib of your partner's mask, under his jaw on the left side of his face ("near the ear" is specified).
5. Step slightly forwards and to the right with your right foot, turning it to point left. Lean back a little.
6. Your point lands on his mask as your foot lands. You are far enough from his blade that it should pose no direct threat (there is no proper opposition). (C)

148

Figure 135 **Scanso del pie dritto** *drill: Tapani (right) stringers Maaret; as she disengages to attack, he strikes while stepping off the line. His blade remains on the far side of hers.*

Alternatively, you can gain more distance in your avoidance, and get further offline, by executing a similar defence with the *scanso della vita*.

Plate 19 *Scanso della vita* drill

1. Partner stands on guard in *terza*
2. Stringer him on the outside. (A)
3. Partner disengages to thrust with a lunge on the inside, in *quarta* (B)
4. Turn your hand to *quarta*, aiming at your partner's mask ("a thrust to the face" is specified).
5. Pass your left foot behind your right foot, throwing your body around and somewhat forwards. Lean into it, away from your partner's blade. Your point lands on his mask a fraction before your foot lands. You are well away from his blade. (C)

Figure 136 Scanso della vita *drill: drill: Maaret (right) stringers Tapani on the outside; as he disengages to attack, she strikes while passing off the line.*

The *scannatura*

This technique is described in detail and illustrated in plate 13, and occurs again in plate 14 as a counter; a technique just like it (though not named as such) appears also on plate 17 as a counter to the *scanso del pie dritto*. It is by all accounts an important technique, though Capo Ferro is frustratingly vague when it comes to defining it. The term itself is translated by Swanger as "butchering"; graphic, but not helpful!

The play begins with you stringering your opponent on the outside, soliciting his attack to your inside line. You then "meet his sword on the outside, lowering the point to seconda, and passing with the left leg in one same tempo strike him in the flank, lowering the hilt with the body and seizing his hand as you see"

The accompanying plate looks like this:

Figure 137 Scannatura, *Capo Ferro original, plate 13 (courtesy Greenhill Books)*

Plate 13 scannatura drill

1. Partner stands on guard in *terza*
2. Stringer him on the outside (A)
3. Partner disengages to thrust with a lunge on the inside, in *quarta* (B)
4. Drop your point over his sword, towards and no lowerthan his waist (C)
5. wedging his blade to the outside with your true edge (D)
6. Pass forwards with the left foot
7. Grasping his sword hand with your left hand while thrusting him in the flank. (E)
8. This action should be done in one fluid motion forwards; the sword parries and thrusts in one action, like a spiral. It is very important to keep your hand forward; do not be tempted to push his sword away by pushing your hilt out to the side. A proper *seconda* is all that's required.

A

B

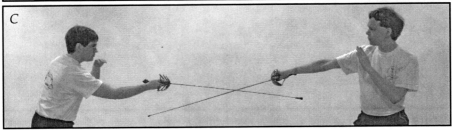

C

Figure 138 *Scannatura drill: Tapani stringers Markku on the outside; as Markku disengages to attack, Tapani drops his point over the blade, transporting it to the outside; and passes in to strike, grasping Markku's sword hand.*

This is a perfect opportunity to complete our study of plate 14: it involves three plays beyond the contratempo example cited above, one of which includes the *scannatura*.

Here they are, in the order laid out by Capo Ferro:

Plate 14 parry-riposte drill

1. Partner stands on guard in *terza* (A)
2. Stringer him on the inside, in *quarta*
3. He disengages and attacks in *terza* to your face (B)
4. As he attacks, lift your point, meeting his sword on the outside
5. Turn your hand to *seconda*, thrust to his chest (C)
6. While passing forwards with the left foot
7. And grasping his sword hand. (D)

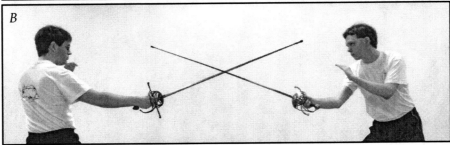

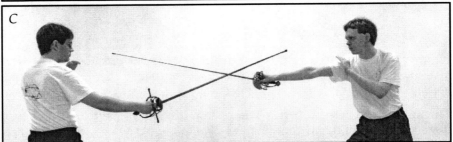

Figure 139 *Plate 14 parry riposte drill: Tapani stringers Markku on the inside; Markku disengages to attack; Tapani parries with the false edge, and strikes in* seconda, *passing in. (Tapani's blade starts on the far side and finishes on this)*

Plate 14 *scannatura* drill

1. Stand on guard in *terza*
2. Partner stringers you on the inside, in *quarta* (A)
3. Disengage and attack in *terza* to his face (B)
4. As you attack, he lowers his point, turns his hand to *seconda*, stepping in a little with the right foot while dropping into *sbasso*. (C)
5. Drop your point towards his waist, turning your hand to *seconda* while (D)
6. Pulling back your right foot,
7. Meeting his sword on the outside, and thrusting to his flank. (E)

Figure 140 *Plate 14 scannatura drill: Tapani is stringered by Markku; as he disengages to attack, Markku tries an attack with a* sbasso; *Tapani pulls back a little, parries in* seconda, *and strikes.*

The final play on plate 14 introduces the defensive uses of the left hand.

Plate 14 hand parry drill

1. Stand on guard in *terza*
2. Partner stringers you on the inside, in *quarta* (A)
3. Disengage and attack in *terza* to his face (B)
4. As you attack, he lowers his point, turns his hand to *seconda*, stepping in a little with the right foot while dropping into *sbasso*. (C)
5. sweep your left hand down under your right arm, parrying his sword to your right, while (D)
6. turning your rapier to *seconda* while
7. Pulling back your right foot,
8. Thrust over your partner's sword, to his chest or face.

Figure 141 *Plate 14 hand parry drill: Tapani (right) stringers Markku, who disengages to attack. Tapani responds by attempting a sbasso; Markku pulls back, parries with his left hand and strikes.*

Feints: counters to the plays

A consistent theme in *Gran Simulacro* is, after presenting a play in the form of "D stringers C, C attacks, D kills him", going on to say "but if C had been clever, or experienced, he would have feinted, and D coming confidently in to kill him, C would have stabbed him like so".

I paraphrase somewhat, but the point is clear; the *stringere* is an action made to gain measure and tempo. The measure is gained; do not give him a tempo! Let him *think* he has a tempo to hit you in, and when he commits himself, teach him the error of his ways.

Capo Ferro devotes one "Admonition" (number 7, "On the vanity of Feints") and one "Explanation" (number 8) to feints. In the Admonition, he effectively states that feints are useless against you if you can judge distance properly: a feint out of measure can be ignored: a feint in measure is a tempo, and you can counterstrike while it occurs.

This would appear to mean that feinting is a waste of effort; in which case why does it occur in so many counters? My feeling is that Capo Ferro is talking about offensive feints: where someone attacks using feints to confuse the opponent. It is a different matter when the feint represents an attack that the opponent thinks he has set you up for. The point made is good, though: if the feint is out of measure a seasoned fencer will ignore it; if it is in measure, it can be a tempo, a time in which to strike. This is also a distinction between the Art and the Use; feints are not perfect as they rely on your opponent being fooled; however in the realm of the use, people often are fooled, so feints work.

The essence of the feint, as Capo Ferro describes it in Explanation 8, is deception: the "deceitful gestures…strike directly at the opposite of that at which they gesture". The idea is to threaten one line, forcing your opponent to cover that line, then strike in the line that is opened by his movement. Here Capo Ferro does not mention whether he approves of these actions or not, it is presumably covered by Admonitions 7, and the Art v. Use distinction mentioned earlier.

Whether Art or Use, though, feints and the deception of parries are a core component of this system, re-occurring throughout the book, though more commonly against parries with the dagger than parries with the sword.

We have already seen the use of feints in the plate 7 parrying drills, in the chapter on parry-ripostes. It would be a good idea now to examine more closely how these feints are done, and to give a few more examples, countering plays you already know.

The purpose of the feint is deception. Your partner must be wholly convinced that your action is a real attack, so he may "approach confidently in order to attack" (plate 7). Yet at the same time you must keep your body "somewhat held back", to remain safe and to give yourself time to execute your counter.

Feinting drill, part one

1. Stand on guard in *terza*
2. partner stringers on the inside in *quarta* (A)
3. disengage and feint in *seconda*, on the outside, keeping your body back. (B)
4. Repeat from step 1, but at step 3, attack. Partner executes a parry riposte (C)
5. repeat, varying randomly whether you attack or feint.
6. Repeat, and see whether you can convince your partner to parry when you are merely feinting.

When you can successfully convince your partner that your feint is an attack, repeat the drill, feint at step 3, and when he parries, disengage, avoiding his sword, change line to *quarta* (you are now on the inside) and strike to his chest. (fig. D)

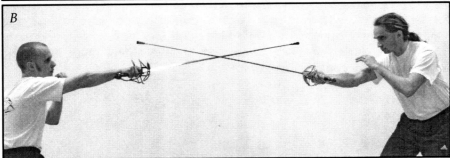

Figure 142 *Feinting drill, part one: Harri (left) is stringered by Petri on the inside. He disengages to feint (B) or strike (C). If Petri tries to parry the feint, Harri disengages in time and strikes in* quarta *(D).*

Feinting drill, part two

1. Stand on guard in *quarta*
2. partner stringers on the outside (A)
3. Disengage and feint in *quarta*, on the inside, keeping your body back. (B)
4. Repeat from step 1, but at step 3, attack. Partner executes a parry riposte. (C)
5. repeat, varying randomly whether you attack or feint.
6. Repeat, and see whether you can convince your partner to parry when you are merely feinting.

When you can successfully convince your partner that your feint is an attack, repeat the drill, feint at step 3, and when he parries, disengage (fig. D), avoiding his sword, change line to *seconda* (you are now on the outside) and strike to his chest. (fig. E)

Figure 146 *Plate 17 second play drill: Maaret (left is stringered on the outside by Tapani, She disengages with a feint, Tapani falls for it and tries a* scanso del pie dritto; *Maaret parries and enters.*

Other options

It would be misleading to suggest that all you can do when finding yourself stringered is disengage and attack, feint, or strike in contratempo, the options so far presented. One of my favourites, for sheer simplicity, is this play from plate 8:

Plate 8, second play drill

1. Stand on guard in *terza*
2. Partner stringers on the inside in *quarta* (A)
3. Attack with a *riverso* to the face (B)
4. Continue with a *mandritto fendente* to the head (C, D)
5. retire in *quarta* (E)

When executing the first cut, be careful to close the line; though Capo Ferro does not mention it, I suggest sidestepping to the right as you do it.

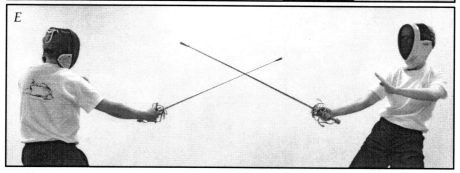

Figure 147 *Plate 8 second play drill: Ilkka stringers Rami on the inside; he responds by disengaging and striking* riverso *and* mandritto *to Ilkka's head.*

Or you can dominate the sword with a strike. "Explanation 13" is entitled "Most Useful Admonition Regarding Dominating the Sword" (not to be confused with the Admonitions) and there Capo Ferro specifies two means of dominating the sword. The first is "when having acquired the adversary's sword, I never quit the domination while striking". This should be very clear to you by now: most of the plays thus far have required you to maintain opposition while attacking.

Secondly, if you beat yuour opponent's sword, while it is moving out of line from the impetus you gave it, it is understood to be under your domination. In other words, when you strike your opponent's sword, you have the time in which it is moving away from you in which to strike. You have already covered the physical action of the strike: it is the same *mezzo mandritto*, or *falso manco* that has served as a parry.

This play from plate 16 shows a similar response to the one seen on plate 9 second play:

Plate 16 second play drill

1. Stand on guard in *quarta*.
2. Partner stringers your sword on the outside. (A)
3. Disengage and strike your partner's sword with a *mezzo mandritto* (B, C, D)
4. Immediately thrust to the face (E)
5. Retire in *terza* (F)

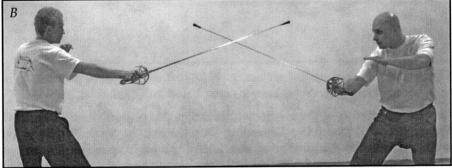

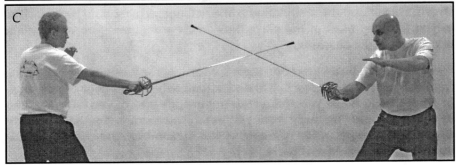

Figure 148 *Plate 16 second play drill: Otto (right) is tsringered on the outside by Ilkka. He responds by disengaging, beating Ilkka's blade with a* mezzo mandritto ordinario, *and thrusting to the face.*

171

Plate 16 third play drill

1. Stand on guard in *quarta*.
2. Partner stringers your sword on the outside. (A)
3. Disengage and strike your partner's sword with a *mezzo mandritto* (B)
4. Immediately cut a *riverso* to his arm (C)
5. Retire in *terza* (D)

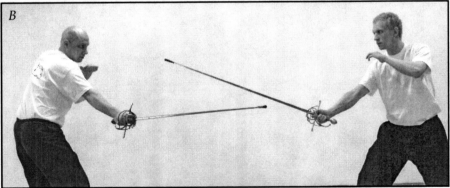

Figure 149 *Plate 16 third play drill: Otto 8right) stringers Ilkka on the outside; Ilkka disenages and beats Otto's blade down; and cuts his arm.*

Be careful during the strike not to expose yourself by too wide an action. Be sure to keep your point offensive at all times; it is the only thing between you and your opponent's intention to kill you.

Chapter 7

The Dagger

The dagger is the classic accompaniment to the rapier. As with most other writers of rapier treatises, Capo Ferro requires that you master the sword alone before adding the dagger. He writes: "You must know that the unaccompanied sword is the queen and foundation of all other weapons, yea, that to delight therein is as, and more useful than, to do so in others".

The function of the dagger is primarily defensive, and while parrying with the dagger, you should strike with the sword (see Admonitions 2). While Capo Ferro may seem a tad dismissive of the dagger (see for example chapter 13, Table, 119) he nonetheless devotes a full 19 plates to its use (compare this to 15 plates of single sword plays, and two each for sword and cape and sword and shield. (This count does not include plate 1 showing the swords about to be drawn, plates 2—4 showing the six guards, all with daggers, nor plate 5 showing the lunge, without a dagger). It is clearly a vital part of the system.

Grip

There are two means of gripping the dagger, both of which can be seen on plate 39: they are the thumb-up and the finger-over.

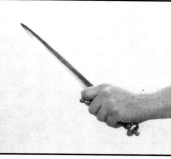

Figure 150
Dagger grip, thumb up

Figure 151
Dagger grip, finger over

Though the thumb-up grip is far more common in general rapier and dagger play, the finger-over is illustrated far more often in this treatise. Given that Capo Ferro makes no mention of how to hold the dagger anywhere, we are forced to rely on the pictures. However, the historical record of daggers designed for the left hand to accompany a rapier, almost invariably shows daggers that have a side ring, which effectively precludes the use of the finger-over grip (or at least forces you to hold the dagger with the ring on the inside, rendering it useless). We must also take into account the anatomical impossibility of the grip on the rapier shown by figure C on plate 6; the plates are not 100% reliable.

I suggest that you attempt all of the plays here with both grips, and find which one works best for you in which circumstance. It is not unreasonable to suppose that the grip may be shifted according to the needs of the fight. This is one point where a purist may disagree with my approach, but I only ever use the thumb-up grip.

Rapier and dagger guards

In addition to the four solo rapier guards, the addition of the dagger gives us two new guards; however it is obvious from the plates that the sword is always in one of the four normal guards; and the dagger is either high and forward, high and back, or low.

The dagger is always pointing forwards or up when in guard.

Prima

Figure 152 *Prima with dagger, Topi demonstrating*

176

Seconda

Figure 153   *Seconda with dagger, Topi demonstrating*

Terza

Figure 154   *Terza with dagger, Topi demonstrating*

177

Quarta

Figure 155   *Quarta with dagger, Topi demonstrating*

Quinta

Figure 156   *Quinta guard, Topi demonstrating*

Sesta

Figure 157 *Sesta guard, Topi demonstrating*

Stringering at sword and dagger

Capo Ferro has two simple rules for stringering at sword and dagger: "if the point of the enemy's sword is aimed towards your right side you will find him on the outside, and moreover that if it occurs to you to stringer the low guards, you will stringer with the sword in the sloping line" (plate 21) He gives no instruction about how to stringer (such as whether to make contact with the blade or not, etc). He also does not refer to stringering with the dagger (though plate 3 appears to show something like it).

Capo Ferro also mentions (on plate 21) the problem that besets all writers of instructional manuals: it is not possible to cover every contingency. Instead, he "defers to the discretion of the reader" … in other words, you are supposed to apply the principles he ahs set down, guided by the examples shown, to work out what to do.

The text reads: "Figures of the sword and dagger which demonstrate the manner of stringering the adversary's sword, he being found in a high prima on the inside" making it clear that D is stringering A, but it appears that the blade relationship is wrong; D should be acquiring A's debole with his forte, but it is the other way round. Capo Ferro does not explain this, but perhaps he is stringering the body only, and is covered by his dagger as he does so.

Figure 158 *Plate 21 (courtesy Greenhill Books)*

In all other ways, stringering the sword appears to be the same when at sword and dagger, as with sword alone.

Parries

Parrying with the dagger can be done to the inside, over or under the sword arm.

Because the dagger is in the left hand, an attack met on the right of the dagger is on the inside; a blade to the left of your dagger is on the outside. This is the reverse of the lines regarding the sword: a parry to the inside of the dagger will take your opponent's blade to the outside of your sword:

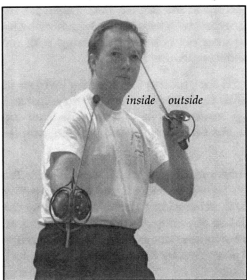

Figure 159 *Inside and outside lines with the dagger (Topi demonstrating)*

The mechanics of parrying with the dagger are very simple. You either push the incoming blade aside with the edge, moving your hand across, or you "windscreen wiper" the dagger to deflect. In effect, either dagger moves as a unit, or it rotates around the grip.

These drills should make it clear. These parrying drills are simplified versions of plays found in *Gran Simulacro*, just to accustom you to using the left hand, and to get you used to letting the dagger take over your defence. Your partner doesn't need a dagger at first. Once you have hang of them, refer to the original source (and the translation if necessary) and recreate them more faithfully. I have included examples of some of these plays done by the book in the sample plays chapter: refer to them if you need help.

Dagger parrying drill one: over the arm (plate 22)

1. Partner stands on guard in *terza*
2. Stringer him quite high on the inside. (A)
3. Your dagger is level with your chest, pointing up.
4. Partner disengages to thrust with a lunge on the outside, in *seconda*
5. meet his sword with your dagger, (B)
   pushing it over your right arm, point high.
6. At the same time, drop your sword point under his sword and thrust to his chest. (C)

This play is based on plate 22, which also shows a thrust to the face and one to the thigh as alternative responses at step 6.

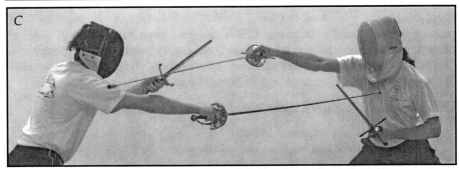

Figure 160 *Dagger parrying drill one: Tapani (left) stringers Petri; Petri disengages to strike; Tapani parries with his dagger and thrusts to Petri's chest.*

Dagger parrying drill two: under the arm (plate 23)

1. Partner stands on guard in *terza*
2. Stringer him quite low on the outside (A)
3. Your dagger is low, pointing forwards
4. Partner disengages to thrust with a lunge on the inside, in *Quarta*
5. Shift your dagger across, meeting his sword and pushing it to the right under your sword arm, (B, C)
6. Which rises to thrust to your partner's face (D)

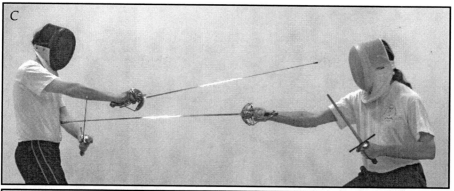

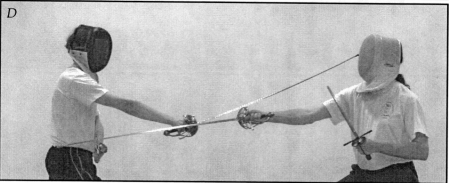

Figure 161 *Dagger parrying drill two under the arm: Tapani (left) stringers Petri; Petri disengages to strike; Tapani parries with his dagger and thrusts to Petri's face.*

Dagger parrying drill three: high outside (plate 27)

1. Partner stands on guard in *terza*
2. Stringer him on the outside, quite high, with your dagger low, as in the *sesta* and *prima* guards. (A)
3. Partner disengages to thrust with a lunge on the inside, in *quarta* (B)
4. Lift your dagger to parry his thrust away and to the left, with the false edge (ref plate 27 etc.)
5. while you thrust him in the chest. (C)

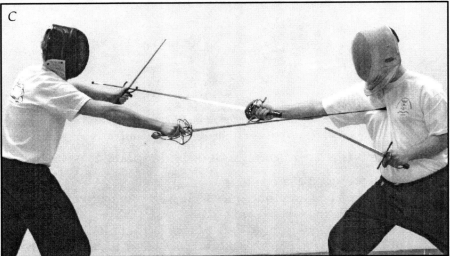

Figure 162 *Dagger parrying drill three, high outside: Ilkka (left) stringers Otto to the outside; as Otto disengages and thrusts, Ilkka parries high with the dagger and strikes.*

Notice that this is the only parry that can reasonably be done with either edge, but Capo Ferro exclusively shows the false edge being used, so we go with that.

Dagger parrying drill four: low outside (plate 32)

1. Partner stands on guard in *terza*
2. Stringer him quite low on the outside, with your dagger high. (A)
3. Partner disengages to thrust with a lunge on the inside, in *Quarta* (B)
4. drop the point of your dagger to parry him away low and to the left, (C)
5. while thrusting him in the chest. (Not shown)

Figure 163 *Dagger parrying drill four, low outside: Antti (left) stringers Topi on the outside: Topi disengages to strike, Antti parries him low, and is about to strike.*

Deceiving the dagger

At rapier and dagger play one of the more common actions is forcing your partner to parry with his dagger, and disengaging or cutting over it as he does so. This will normally be done while parrying with your own dagger at the same time; it is a good idea to master the basic skill first before multitasking. In these drills your partner will not attack, so you don't have to worry about using your dagger to parry while working out the deception. This is unrealistic, but is a necessary build-up to the full technique.

Dagger deception drill one: over the arm (Plate 23)

1. Stand on guard in *terza*
2. Your partner stringers you quite high on the inside (A)
3. His dagger is level with his chest, pointing up.
4. Disengage to thrust with a lunge on the outside, in *seconda* (B)
5. as his dagger comes across to parry over his arm (C), cut over with your point, and thrust. (E)

Figure 164 *Dagger deception drill one: Antti (left) stringers Topi on the inside; Topi disengages; Antti starts to parry; Topi cuts over and strikes.*

Dagger deception drill two: under the arm

1. Stand on guard in *terza*
2. Your partner stringers you quite low on the outside (A)
3. His dagger is low, pointing forwards
4. Disengage to thrust with a lunge on the inside, in *quarta* (B)
5. Partner shifts his dagger across, to parry under his arm (C)
6. Disengage under his dagger (D) and thrust him in the chest. (E)

Figure 165 *Dagger deception drill two: under the arm: Antti (left) stringers Topi on the outside; Topi disengages; Antti starts to parry; Topi disengages under and strikes.*

Dagger deception drill three: high outside (plate 27)

1. Stand on guard in *terza*
2. Partner stringers you on the outside, quite high, with his dagger low, as in the *sesta* and *prima* guards. (A)
3. Disengage anticlockwise to thrust with a lunge on the inside, in *quarta* (B)
4. As he lifts his dagger to parry, (C)
5. Disengage clockwise and thrust him in the chest. (D)

Note that simply turning your hand from *quarta* to *seconda* makes for a perfect disengage over the dagger.

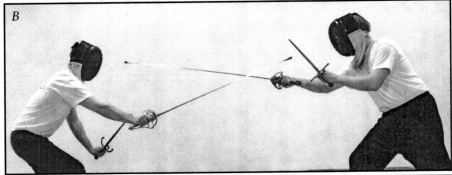

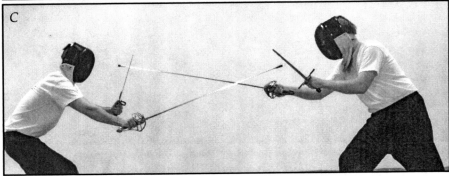

Figure 166 *Dagger deception drill three, high outside: Antti (left) stringers Topi on the outside; Topi disengages; Antti starts to parry; Topi disengages over and strikes in seconda.*

Dagger deception drill four: low outside (plate 30)

1. Stand on guard in *terza*
2. Partner stringers you quite low on the outside, with his dagger high. (A)
3. Disengage to thrust with a lunge on the inside, in *Quarta* (B)
4. Partner drops the point of his dagger to parry, (C)
5. Disengage anticlockwise over his dagger and
6. Thrust him in the chest. (D)

Figure 167 *Dagger deception drill four, low outside: Antti (left) stringers Topi on the outside; Topi disengages; Antti starts to parry; Topi disengages over and strikes in* seconda.

When deceiving the dagger you should avoid his parry completely, so that there is no contact between his dagger and your blade. Notice of course that these drills are arranged as the reverse of the previous dagger parrying drills; and remember that all the rules of single rapier play still apply, such as striking according to the point, entering cautiously to stringer, etc.

In the above drills, you deceive the dagger with a feint. In all such drills you run the risk of walking onto your partner's point. This is prevented by your dagger: as you strike him, you should always have his sword under control, usually with your dagger, sometimes with your sword.

A closer look at plate 22 will reinforce the concept. Here is the play, step by step.

Plate 22 drill 1: dagger deception by feint

1. Partner stands on guard in *sesta*
2. approach from the outside in terza, threatening his face. (A)
3. Convinced by his passivity, attack with a thrust to his face.
4. Partner parries with the dagger, high and to the outside.
5. While thrusting you in the face. (B)

This sets up the logic behind your partner's actions.

1. repeat the drill, but at step 3, feint to his face,
2. as he parries, deceive it, lifting your point over his dagger
3. and thrusting him in the face in *seconda*,
4. while parrying his thrust under your sword arm. (C)

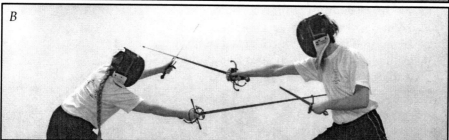

Figure 168 *Plate 22 drill one: Tapani (right) threatens Maaret (left); B: Maaret parries and strikes (Tapani has parried, beyond the drill); C: Tapani has parried, and deceived Maaret's parry, striking Maaret's mask.*

193

So now you can go back and repeat all the drills above, simply adding the appropriate dagger parry whenever your partner is supposed to thrust. If he is supposed to stand still, then simply cover his sword with your dagger.

The basic rule of thumb when parrying with the dagger is to go by the shortest route. If his blade comes inside your dagger, above your sword arm,, parry over your arm to the right. If it comes in below your sword arm and under your dagger arm, parry down and out. So, how you parry depends on where your dagger is to begin with, and where the attack is coming to.

Staying with plate 22, for example, we can see your striking options after (or more properly during) a successful parry with the dagger over your sword arm. The text describes when to strike the face, the chest or the thigh. If he has attacked your face, the line to his head, chest and thigh are open. If he has attacked your chest, the position of his sword and arm will be a little different (his arm will be a little lower, see the photographs for details), which effectively precludes an attack to his chest. The aim of this plate is therefore to point out that you can strike to a range of targets, and also to remind you that those targets are restricted by his position.

You can drill this sequence like so:

Plate 22, drill 2

1. Repeat dagger parrying drill one:
2. Partner stands on guard in *terza*
3. Stringer him quite high on the inside. (A)
4. Your dagger is level with your chest, pointing up.
5. Partner disengages to thrust with a lunge on the outside, in *seconda*. Because you have stringered high, he aims at your face.
6. Meet his sword with your dagger, pushing it over your right arm, point high.
7. At the same time, drop your point under his sword and thrust to his chest. (B)

Figure 169 *Plate 22, drill two: Maaret (left) stringers Tapani on the inside; as he attacks, she parries with her dagger, avoids his dagger, and strikes his chest.*

Now, repeat the drill like so:

Plate 22, drill 3

1. Partner stands on guard in *terza*
2. Stringer him quite high on the inside. (A)
3. Your dagger is level with your chest, pointing up.
4. Partner disengages to thrust with a lunge on the outside, in *seconda*. Because you have stringered high, he aims at your face.
5. Meet his sword with your dagger, pushing it over your right arm, point high.
6. At the same time, drop your sword point under his sword and thrust to his thigh. (B)

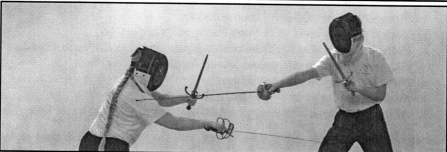

Figure 170 *Plate 22, drill three: Maaret (left) stringers Tapani on the inside; as he attacks, she parries with her dagger, and strikes his thigh.*

And again, like so:

Plate 22, drill 4

1. Partner stands on guard in *terza*
2. Stringer him quite high on the inside.
3. Your dagger is level with your chest, pointing up.
4. Partner disengages to thrust with a lunge on the outside, in *seconda*. Because you have stringered high, he aims at your face.
5. Meet his sword with your dagger, pushing it over your right arm, point high.
6. At the same time, aim your point at his mask and thrust to his face.

Figure 171 *Plate 22, drill four: Tapani (right) has attacked; Maaret parries with her dagger and thrusts at his mask.*

And again, but this time change the height of your point when you stringer to invite a thrust to the chest:

Plate 22, drill 5

1. Partner stands on guard in *terza*
2. Stringer him at mid-level on the inside.
3. Your dagger is level with your chest, pointing up. (A)
4. Partner disengages to thrust with a lunge on the outside, in *seconda*. Because you have stringered lower, he aims at your chest. (B)
5. Meet his sword with your dagger, pushing it over your right arm, point high.
6. At the same time, aim your point at his mask and thrust to his face. (C)

Notice that because his arm is a bit lower, you don't have a clear shot at his chest.

Figure 172 *Plate 22, drill five: Maaret (left) stringers Tapani on the inside; as he attacks, she parries with her dagger, and strikes his mask.*

197

And again, like so:

Plate 22, drill 6

1. Partner stands on guard in *terza*
2. Stringer him at mid-level on the inside.
3. Your dagger is level with your chest, pointing up.
4. Partner disengages to thrust with a lunge on the outside, in *seconda*. Because you have stringered lower, he aims at your chest.
5. Meet his sword with your dagger, pushing it over your right arm, point high.
6. At the same time, drop your sword point under his sword and thrust to his thigh.

Figure 173   Tapani (right) has attacked; Maaret parries with her dagger and thrusts at his leg.

You will have noticed by now that every time there is a decision tree, a point where you have more than one option, I have taken the trouble to write out and illustrate a whole new drill, to make sure that the options are all practised. This is so that you come to instinctively recognise how you can limit your opponent's options, and what changes in his technique occasion changes in yours. It is very important in my opinion not to skip over the repetitive parts of these drill sequences. One of the main tactical tools your opponent has is to condition your responses, to predict what you will do under certain stimuli. You must understand this process to guard against it, and you must also learn to recognise how small changes early in a sequence can quite radically alter the final outcome. Rapier is in my opinion a weapon ideally suited for nit-picking, pedantic perfectionist control freaks. Cultivate these character traits for best results!

Sample plays

Now that you have the basic idea of how Capo Ferro would have you use the dagger, I will take you through some of the plays, selected more for their variety than for their similarities. This is to show you how broad the system really is; once the basic principles are understood, and the basic actions mastered, there is an amazing array of applications available. It is beyond the scope of this book to go through every single plate and play that Capo Ferro presents; I have tried to extract the key plays so that when you go and do your own, complete, interpretation you will have encountered all the main concepts here.

Plate 29

This plate covers the pre-emptive use of the dagger; not to parry, but to cover yourself against a potential attack. In it you respond to the stringering with a beat, and cover yourself with your dagger as you attack. I interpret the play like so:

Plate 29 drill

1. Stand on guard in *terza*, with the dagger crossed over your forte
2. Your partner comes to stringer you on the outside. (A)
3. **Disengage and beat his debole firmly with a** *mezzo mandritto* (B)
4. Cover his blade with your dagger; don't reach for it, just keep your dagger between his blade and you.
5. At the same time, push your point towards his chest, turning your hand to *seconda* (**this is shown in the figure). This angles your blade** around his dagger, making it much harder for him to parry in time.
6. As you attack, his blade will naturally recover from the beat, and threaten you. Parry this with your dagger. (C)

Figure 174 *Plate 29 beat attack: Otto (left) stringers Ilkka, who disengages and strikes Otto's blade with a mezzo mandritto, and attacks, covering Otto's sword with his dagger.*

Plate 32

This plate includes my favourite dagger parry (don't ask me why, I just like it), and simultaneously feinting against his dagger.

Plate 32 drill

1. Partner stands on guard in a high terza, with his dagger "crossed and joined at the beginning of the forte"
2. Come to stringer on the outside, with your dagger high. (A)
3. Partner disengages, sets aside your blade with his dagger (as in a high outside parry) and thrusts (all this in one tempo) (B)
4. Parry by dropping the point of your dagger over his sword (refer to dagger parrying drill 4), disengaging under his dagger, and thrusting in quarta to his face "or wherever it happens to be more convenient". (C)

Figure 175 *Plate 32 drill: Rami (right)stringers Janne, who disengages to strike; Rami parries, avoids Janne's dagger, and strikes Janne's mask.*

If you compare the casual instruction to strike "wherever it happens to be more convenient" in this plate with the careful laying out of options in plate 22, we can see that the author is expecting his readers to remember what has gone before; to be able to identify "convenient" targets.

Plate 33

This plate includes further tactical uses of shifting the right leg back. We have encountered this concept before in the plays of plate 8, but the application here is quite different.

Work through the play, and then compare with the plate 8 drill.

Plate 33 drill

1. Partner stands on guard in low terza
2. Adopt a high terza "with your dagger joined crossed over your forte" (A)
3. He attacks in seconda over your dagger with a pass, "parrying wide" with his dagger. (B)
4. As he enters, pass back with your right leg, to gain time, parrying with your dagger to the high outside (Capo Ferro doesn't mention the parry, but the plate clearly shows it, and common sense demands it)
5. while deceiving his dagger with a disengagement underneath it,
6. and pushing your weight forward to strike,
   turning your hand to *quarta*. (C)

A

Figure 176 *Plate 33 pass back: Markku (left) awaits Tapani's attack; it comes; and Markku passes back, deceiving Tapani's dagger and parrying with his own.*

Plate 38: left hander

I have included this play as it is one of the few examples in a rapier text of what to do against a left-hander. The techniques themselves are not remarkable, but the context in which they are being used is.

If you don't have a left-handed partner, one of you should switch hands for this drill, it does work quite differently. The left hander can repeat the exact same drill with the directions reversed, as usual. Capo Ferro gives this situation only one simple set-up, and three plays. I have reversed the order of the plays to fit better with the order in which you have seen the techniques before.

Plate 38, drill 1

1. Left-handed partner on guard in *quarta*.
2. Come to stringer his inside in *terza* (as if stringering a right-hander on the outside). (A)
3. Partner disengages and attacks in *seconda*,
4. Close the line with *quarta*, and strike. (B)

Figure 177 *Plate 38, drill one: Tapani (right) stringers Antti Roivanen on the inside; as Antti disengages to strike, Tapani closes the line with quarta and strikes.*

Plate 38, drill 2

1. Left-handed partner on guard in *quarta*.
2. Come to stringer his inside in *terza*
   (as if stringering a right-hander on the outside).
3. Partner disengages and attacks in *seconda*,
4. Lower your dagger to parry him under your sword arm,
5. while striking him in the chest in *seconda*.

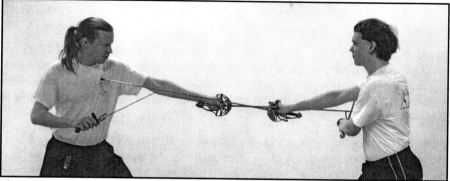

Figure 178   *Plate 38 drill 2: Antti (left) has disengaged to strike; Tapani parries with his dagger, and thrusts.*

Plate 38, drill 3

1. Left-handed partner on guard in *quarta*.
2. Come to stringer his inside in *terza*
   (as if stringering a right-hander on the outside).
3. Partner disengages and attacks in *seconda*,
4. Lower your dagger to parry him under your sword arm,
5. while turning a *stramazzone riverso* to his face.

Figure 179   *Plate 38 drill 3: Antti (left) has disengaged to strike; Tapani parries with his dagger, and cuts* stramazzone riverso.

Plate 39: the cross parry

Capo Ferro introduces this classic technique of stage, screen, and historical fencing, the parry with the dagger and sword crossed above the head, with these immortal words:

> Harbi certamente fatto torto a me medesimo, se cosi nobil parata, o vero difesa, io non vi havesse discoperto, la qual difende, salua cosi nobil parte della vita.

> (I would certainly have wronged myself if I had not revealed to you this noble parry, or defence, which defends, and saves such a noble part of the body.)

And I will not so wrong myself as to leave it out either. This also gives me an excellent opportunity to show how a reader's assumptions can get in the way of good interpretation. After describing how this should be done according to the text, I'll describe my initial misconceptions that lead me at first to get this play completely wrong.

Capo Ferro does not appear to use a crossed parry except to protect the head. The text accompanying the plate is unusually indistinct; instead of calling each fencer by the letter associated with him (as in most other plates), he says:

> I put forth to you the present figures, of whom one lies in prima, and the other in quinta; and from quinta, only by raising his arm and turning his hand into quarta, increasing the pace, he will have come to gain the sword of the adversary on the inside, and the enemy disengaging by turning under his enemy's sword, he will have thrown a dritto fendente at the same, but the same only by turning his hand into seconda with the point high, putting the dagger to the rear on the forte of his sword, will be able to strike the adversary safely in two places: with a thrust in the face, or a cut to the leg.

Carefully navigating the syntax I interpret this like so:

Plate 39 drill

1. You are on guard in *quinta*
2. Your partner stands on guard in *prima* (A)
3. Enter in *quarta*, stringering his sword (B)
4. As you enter, partner disengages and cuts *dritto fendente* at your head (C)
5. Turn your sword to *seconda*, keeping your point high, and crossing your dagger *behind* your sword. Parry the cut on your forte; your dagger is below his sword, preventing him from coming back around. (D)
6. Using your dagger, keep contact with his sword
7. While riposting with a thrust at his head, from the outside. (E)
8. Repeat the drill, and at step 7, cut to his thigh instead. (F)

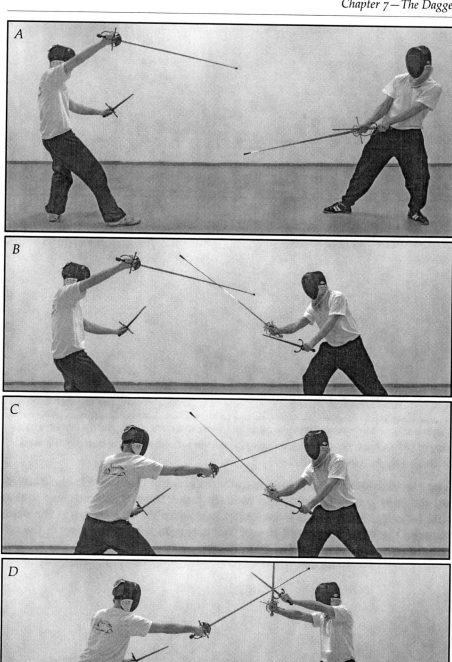

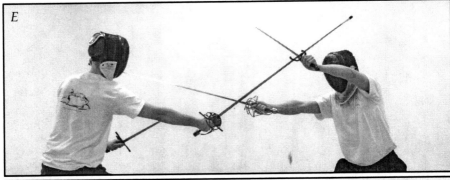

Figure 180 *Plate 39 cross parry drill: Ilkka (right) stringers Antti; Antti disengages; and cuts to Ilkka's head. Ilkka parries, crossing his dagger behind; and thrusts at Antti's mask. Alternatively, he cuts at Antti's leg.*

The way this parry is executed is quite different to that done in the movies, on stage, or generally execute in modern rapier fencing. So much so that at first I thought there was a mistake in Capo Ferro's text: a glance at the plate showed me what I expected to see: the dagger *in front of* the sword, the cut caught between sword and dagger, like so:

Figure 181 *Ilkka and Antti demonstrate the "Common" cross parry, dagger in front*

This allows you to control his sword with your dagger while bringing your sword around in a nice big visible long tempo cut to his head:

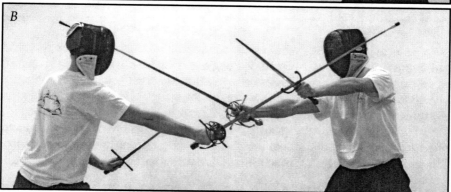

Figure 182 *"Common" cross parry and riposte; Ilkka cuts around at Antti's head.*

Which is splendid, the crowd can see it, it looks great, but your opponent also has all the time in the world to parry it with his dagger, enter, or do any number of equally unpleasant things.

Figure 183
"Common" cross parry countered; Antti parries Ilkka's cut with contemptuous ease and punishes him for stage fighting.

Capo Ferro's version, however, allows you to stay on the outside, taking a much shorter line to the target: less visible to everyone (including your opponent), much faster, and safer. Any doubt about how Capo Ferro is doing it can be cleared up by a closer look at the picture, which supports the text:

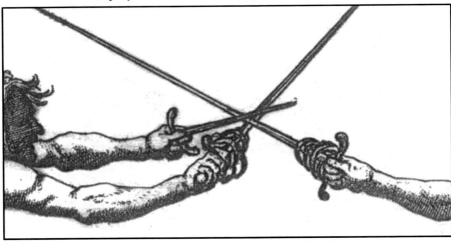

Figure 184   *Plate 39 Cross parry close-up (courtesy Greenhill Books)*

As a general rule, we see what we expect to see; it takes some attention, and willingness to be proved wrong, to repair the inevitable errors that creep in to any interpretation. In this sense, any prior experience of swordsmanship before coming to a treatise is a mixed blessing. On the one hand, the experience may really help you work out how to do any particular play, and give you a handle on the principles at work. But it may also lead you to overlook the details that make the text in hand different to your experience. The proverbial empty cup is an essential requirement of good interpretation.

Out of interest, let us have a look at how this "noble" parry is done by other masters. Fabris, for example, shows us two versions in his *Scienza d'Arme*, on plates 76 and 78 (Leoni, pages 123, 124). It would be inappropriate to set out the plays as drills here because to properly execute them in the Fabrisian manner, one has to use Fabris' guard positions, his exact way of gaining the sword, etc. This would require about another 100 pages of text, 200 photographs, and a year's training on your part in this style. However, the basics are close enough that you should have no trouble walking through the plays in your head and understanding the basic sequence.

In the first example, the play goes like this:

1. You stringer your opponent on the outside;
2. As you enter, your opponent turns a *mandritto* to your head
3. Which you parry by joining "the hilts of sword and dagger and raising [your] hands in a cross" (Leoni page 122). The dagger is in this case in front of and underneath the sword, which is in *seconda*,
4. And you immediately thrust in *prima* over the sword arm.

Figure 185 *Fabris plate 76 cross parry (courtesy Tommaso Leoni)*

In the second example, the play runs:

1. Opponent stands in *quarta* "with the dagger extended and the weapons open" (Leoni 124)
2. You stringer on the inside with the sword and dagger together.
3. Opponent turns a *riverso* at your head as you enter.
4. You "merely turn [your] hands and lean your dagger against your sword" (Leoni 124) to parry. The dagger is again under and in front of the sword.
5. And you immediately thrust to the outside, parrying and striking in the same tempo.

Figure 186 *Fabris cross parry plate 78 (courtesy Tommaso Leoni)*

Fabris gives characteristically complete and detailed explanation of the pros and cons: regarding the cross parry he explains that it is "very strong", "defends the head on both sides simultaneously", the "only drawback is that it offers a limited reach in the counter" (Leoni 122).

Looking at these plays, we can see that Fabris does this parry quite differently to Capo Ferro; the dagger is on the other side of the sword, and the point of contact in the parry is different. The context is the same (at least in plate 76); you have stringered on the outside, your opponent attacks with a mandritto cut to the head. This leads me to believe that either way of executing the parry can be correct, if the accompanying strike is done in tempo. However, we must at all times be clear as to which master we are following.

Plate 40, strike with dagger and sword

One of the stranger misconceptions I have encountered in my time in Western swordsmanship is the notion that it was "against the rules" to strike with the dagger when duelling at rapier and dagger. While this is a typical example of a romanticizing of the past, it makes absolutely no sense in a martial context, and it is with no surprise that I find dagger attacks in the historical record.

Capo Ferro shows the offensive use of the dagger in plates 40 and 41. Of course, the dagger's primary function is defensive; however, when your left side goes forward for whatever (valid) reason, your dagger is in range of his target.

The text to this plate begins with a charming bit of encouragement:

> Because to some, seeing this following figure struck with the sword and also with the dagger, it will perhaps appear difficult, nevertheless putting the same technique to the test, it will turn out to be easy considering the representation (plate 40)

This play begins in an unusual situation: you are both in *quarta*, and the blades are touching, and both points are aimed at the opponent's face.

Plate 40 drill

1. Both come on guard in *terza* out of measure (A)
2. Enter carefully into measure, changing guard to *quarta*, making contact at the debole true edge to true edge. (B)
3. Apply a sharp pressure to your partner's sword, creating an opening. (C)
4. He turns a riverso to your lead thigh (D)
5. As he does so, parry by dropping your hand in terza, (E)
6. passing forwards with your left leg
7. While thrusting at his rear thigh with your sword (F)
8. and striking over his sword arm with your dagger. (G)

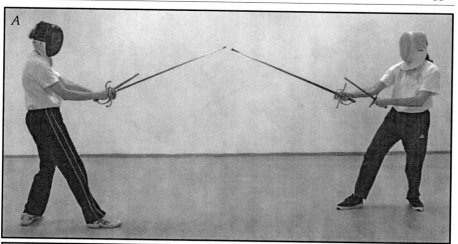

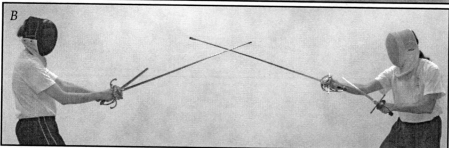

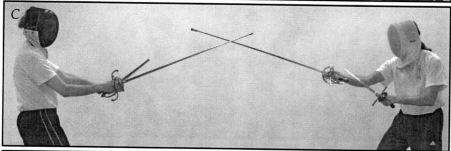

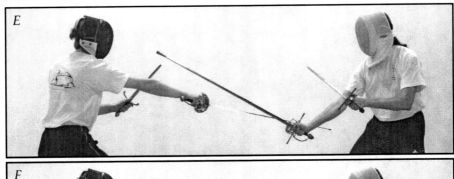

Figure 187 *Plate 40 drill thrust with sword and dagger: Petri (right) enters and pressures Tapani's sword on the inside; Tapani turns a riverso to Petri's leg; Petri parries, and thrusts with both sword and dagger.*

Plate 41, thrust with dagger alone

It is of course also possible to attack with just the dagger if your sword is busy in defence. This plate contains several plays, and a great deal of useful information.

Interestingly, in a break from the usual format, Capo Ferro describes the illustrated play last, and precedes it with several actions. We'll walk through the entirety step by step, beginning with a useful defence, which was thought to be "of great account" by Capo Ferro. Simply, when your opponent thrusts, parry it to the inside or outside as necessary, and return a stramazzone riverso to his arm. There is no mention in the text of how you get to the thrust itself, so I will set up the drill with the usual stringering.

Plate 41 drill 1 A

1. Partner on guard in *terza*.
2. Stringer on the inside with *quarta* (A)
3. Partner takes the tempo and thrusts over your arm in *seconda* (B)
4. Parry this over your arm with the dagger while (C)
5. Turning a stramazzone to his arm. (D)

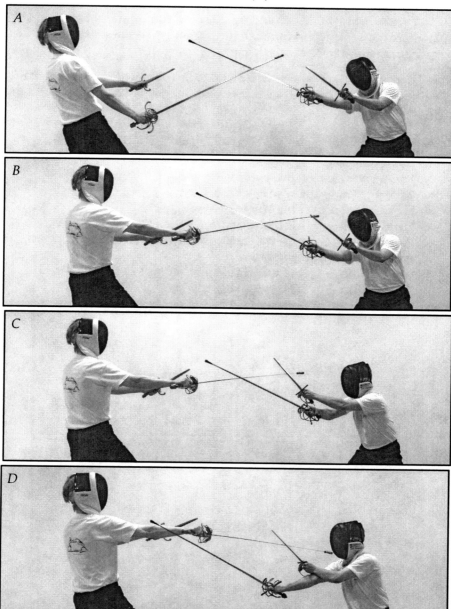

Figure 188 *Plate 41 drill 1 cut to arm: Harri (right) stringers Rami on the inside; Rami pushes through; Harri parries and cuts to the arm.*

Capo Ferro doesn't mention it, but I would be inclined to sidestep a little with your left foot to the left, followed by your right foot in the same direction, as you parry. Try it and see for yourself.

Plate 41 drill 1 B

1. Partner on guard in *terza*.
2. Stringer on the inside with *quarta*
3. Partner takes the tempo and thrusts over your arm in *seconda*
4. Parry this over your arm with the dagger while sidestepping left
5. Turning a stramazzone to his arm.

This defence is the tactical problem that is to be countered in the plays of this plate. So, now reset the drill (either version A or B as you prefer), with the roles reversed.

Plate 41 drill 2

1. Come on guard in *terza*.
2. Partner stringers on the inside with *quarta*
3. Take the tempo and thrusts over his arm in *seconda*
4. He parries this over his arm with his dagger (A)
5. Turning a stramazzone to your arm
6. Parry the stramazzone by turning your hand to meet the sword, parrying in a form of *terza*
7. while passing forward and thrusting over his sword with the dagger. (B)

Figure 189 *Plate 41 drill 2 defence against stramazzone: Harri (right) has stringered Rami, who strikes over the sword, Harri parries and tries to cut; Rami parries and enters, stabbing Harri with his dagger.*

Now we come to the play that is actually illustrated. I find this play particularly interesting as you appear to have to parry with your point way off line, in apparent contradiction to the usual rules. This case is set up for you step by step by Capo Ferro, beginning with what guard positions you are both in, and finishing with a follow-up strike and even specifying which guard you should finish in. We'll do it by the book.

Plate 41 drill 3

1. Partner is on guard in *terza* with the dagger "upon the forte of his sword"
2. Come on guard in *sesta* "with the dagger arm extended forward and the sword somewhat withdrawn" (A)
3. Enter into measure, and thrust over your partner's dagger. (B)
4. Partner parries to the high outside with his dagger (C)
5. and attacks you with the *stramazzone riverso*
6. Parry the *stramazzone* in *quarta* catching it on the hilt of your sword (D)
7. while passing forwards and striking with the dagger under his sword arm. (E)
8. Recover by passing back with the left leg
9. and turning a *riverso* to his sword arm (F)
10. returning to *sesta*. (G)

A

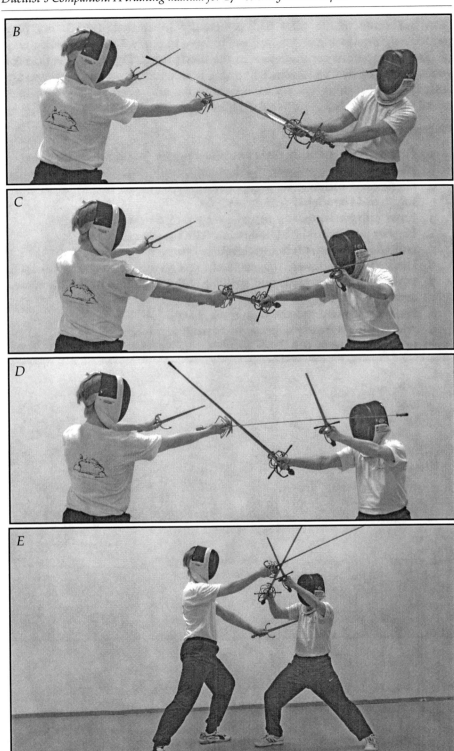

Figure 190 *Plate 41 drill 3: Rami (left) thrusts over Harri's dagger; Harri parries and cuts; Rami parries, and while his sword is tied up, passes in and stabs Harri in the chest; then passes back and cuts his arm (just in case); the stab must have been a lucky shot to a the aorta or the heart as it was expanding causing catastrophic loss of blood pressure to the brain and near-instant collapse. Normally expect a chest-stab victim to keep fighting for many minutes (hence the disabling cut to the arm, ideally severing the tendons that keep the hand closed, making your man unable to hold the sword).*

Parries with the left hand

As we saw in the plate 14 hand parry drill, dagger parries can of course be done with the empty hand (I recommend a sturdy glove just in case). Saviolo, in *His Practice* (1595) discusses this. His pupil (L.) asks:

> L. But I praye you tell me, is it not better to breake with the Swoorde, then with the hand? for (me thinketh) it should be dangerous for hurting the hand.

To which Saviolo (V.) replies:

> V. I will tell you, this weapon must bee used with a glove, and if a man should be without a glove, it were better to hazard a little hurt of the hand, thereby to become maister of his enemies Swoorde, than to breake with the sword, and so give his enemy the advantage of him. (Saviolo, 16)

Saviolo in general prefers to parry with the hand or dagger, leaving the sword for offence only (in this Capo Ferro would disagree, but the latest research on Saviolo suggests that his system was predominantly Spanish, so we should not be surprised by such differences. See Hand and Martinez's article in Spada 1, pages 132–149). However, the point is that dagger parries work well with just the hand, and in free fencing with the single rapier it is perfectly acceptable, advisable and good practice to allow hand parries. So go back and practice all the above dagger parrying drills and dagger deception drills without the dagger.

In fairness I should mention that Fabris is opposed to reliance on the left hand (unarmed) for defence; he describes basing your defence on your left hand as "truly abysmal", and suggests that it is better to only use the left hand to grasp the opponent's hilt, or when getting into grappling (Leoni, page 14). He counsels the fencer to "parry with the sword and make a counter, but at the same time, place the off-hand so as to protect the most likely opening" (Leoni, page 15).

I suspect that Capo Ferro would also consider using the left hand alone to parry contrary to the Art, but part of the Use; likewise, I think they are a necessary part of the fencer's education.

Chapter 8

Theory Summary

The basic concepts of Capo Ferro's fencing system as I see them are these: tempo, measure, and line.[1] To be safe, you must only make sure that the distance you must travel to defend yourself is shorter than that of your opponent's attack; and you must make sure that the line to your target is always closed when in measure. Every action you make is a tempo, an opportunity for your opponent to strike you; likewise every movement he makes in measure is an opportunity for you to strike him. Make certain that when in measure your tempi are shorter than his, and that your forte opposes his debole, and in theory at least, all will be well.

Now that you have encountered all the basic theory in it's physical context, and can execute the plays that exemplify the theory, you may find the following discussion of the terms useful.

Tempo

We have seen that Capo Ferro uses the term tempo to define the length of your own actions, and to denote an opportunity to strike your opponent as he moves. "Tempo" is the measure of motion and stillness. As Capo Ferro writes: "chiefly it signifies a just length of motion or of stillness that I need in order to reach a definite end for some plan of mine" (Table, 50) "Next this word 'tempo' is taken in the sense of quickness, in respect of the length or brevity of the motion or of the stillness" (Table 51). So, "Tempo is not other than the measure of the stillness and of the motion" (Table 53). As we have already seen, when related to an opponent, he qualifies tempo as primo tempo, dui tempi, mezzo tempo and contratempo.

Readers may find it interesting to relate Capo Ferro's use of the term tempo with previous sources. Viggiani, for example considers a full tempo to be a full cut, completely traversing the target. He states (on page 64R)

> Thus a full tempo is a full perfect blow, because that would be a perfect motion and tempo. And a *mezo tempo* would then be … a *mezo mandritto*.[2]

By following his instructions further on in the text, we can see that a full blow traverses the target completely: for example, a transition between guards 3 (held high over the right shoulder, point back, page 69V) and 4 (held low, inside the right foot, point down and forwards, page 71V) constitutes a descending blow (*mandritto sgualembrato*, see page 56V), and a complete tempo. So, Viggiani uses Aristotle's definitions of time and motion (see *Physics* 7 and 8) to describe fencing actions, and the action that he chooses to define tempo by is the full blow.

The *mezzo tempo* definition is also interesting. With Viggiani, the *mezo tempo*[3] is a half blow; his *mezo mandritto* is done by transitioning between guard 3 and guard 5 (page 72V), which is held with the point aimed at the opponent (a similar position to Capo Ferro's *quarta*).

A comparison of Viggiani's definition of tempo relative to movement and stillness (Page 63 Recto, chapter 55) with Capo Ferro's Chapter V, Table 50–60 shows an almost perfect overlap. However, for Capo Ferro, the defining action is the strike at narrow measure of the fixed foot.

Tempo is clearly being used by both Capo Ferro and Viggiani to measure motion. It is also used to define the time in which to strike. Capo Ferro is explicit and precise on this point, and defines five different occasions in which your opponent may give you the tempo:

> The first is when the enemy is fixed in guard, and he lifts or moves his foot that he has forward, that is one tempo in which to accost him; another is when you have parried a blow, then there is a tempo; the third, as he moves himself without judgment from one guard in order to go into another, before he has fixed himself in it, it is a tempo to offend him; and moreover it is tempo when he raises his sword, as he raises his hand, that is a tempo to strike him; and the last is that, when a blow will have travelled past your body, that is a tempo to follow it with a response. (Explanations 5)

If we see what Fabris has to say we find a characteristically simple, clear explanation:

> A tempo is a movement that the opponent makes within the measures … "tempo" also implies an occasion to wound or at least to take some advantage over the opponent. (Leoni, 17)

Let us also take a look at Fabris' use of the term *contratempo*:

> It is important to admonish you that there are some who astutely make a tempo to lure you to attack, and as you do so, they will have parried and countered your blow. This is called wounding in contratempo. Actually, every time you counter an attack (or are the victim of a counter), it is called a contratempo. (Leoni 18)

This is quite different to Capo Ferro, who uses the term more specifically: "Contratempo is when at the very same time that the adversary wants to strike me, I encounter him in shorter tempo and measure" (Explanations 3).

The point I am trying to make with these examples is simply this; we must be aware of the mutation of terms from one treatise to another. Different weapons, and different styles of movement, tend to generate different concepts of time, though the underlying theory of how time is defined may be the same. And even when the weapons and context are almost identical, there will always be differences of opinion on fencing theory and terms for as long as we have fencing masters. It is therefore vital that when discussing Capo Ferro, we use the terminology as he does, while being aware of its differing usage in other systems by other masters.

In summary, Capo Ferro uses tempo to describe any motion or period of stillness on your part or your adversary's; any motion in measure can be an opportunity to strike. Tempo is also used to describe the length of a motion: a lunge is a tempo and a half: simply extending the arm is a mezzo (half) tempo. Any two actions together are two tempi (such as a parry followed by a riposte). Contratempo describes the timing when you defend against an attack: as he comes to strike, you hit him with a shorter action. It is interesting to note that according to Aristotle's definition of tempo, as used by Viggiani and Capo Ferro, the concept of a tempo and a half is nonsense. Either Capo Ferro didn't perfectly understand the Aristotelian notion of tempo, which I find hard to believe, or he was having a bit of a joke, calling a longer tempo a tempo and a half, and a shorter tempo a half tempo.

Measure

Capo Ferro takes some pains to be precise regarding measure:

> Measure is taken for a certain distance from one end to the other, as for example in the art of fencing is taken for the distance that runs from the point of my sword to the body of the adversary, which is wide or narrow (Table 43)

> The measure is a just distance from the point of my sword to the body of my adversary in which I can strike him, according to which all the actions of my sword and defence are given direction.(Table 44)

We have already seen how measure can be measured by tempo; a longer measure requires a longer tempo to cross. Wide measure for example, crossed with a lunge, takes a tempo and a half. In addition, it is necessary when fencing to gain the measure; to get close enough to strike safely. Given the discussion of tempo above, it is unsurprising that Capo Ferro gives us three ways to seek measure:

> I seek it either while I move and the adversary fixes himself, or when I fix myself and the adversary moves, or when I move and the adversary moves (table 106)

Once in range to strike, hence "in measure", the measure is subdivided into three: wide measure (also called by Capo Ferro narrow measure of the increased foot), narrow measure of the fixed foot, and narrow measure of the arm. These take a tempo and a half, a full tempo, and a half tempo to cross respectively.

Stringering

Stringering is an offensive action in which you enter into measure while covering yourself with your sword, your forte opposing his debole. This constrains his sword; he cannot simply attack without first changing the blade relationship: he is therefore forced to attack in two tempi (a cavazione followed by an attack), or in one longer tempo (a cavazione seamlessly developing into an attack). In either case, he is forced into using a longer attack. Therefore stringering an opponent makes his action predictable, and also forces him to use a longer tempo in attack, thus allowing you to counter him in a shorter tempo. Thus by entering into measure by stringering, you acquire a position of tactical superiority. Of course, your entry into measure is in itself a tempo, and your stringering will normally be countered by either a) a cavazione and step back; b) a cavazione and attack; or c) a domination of your sword by a change of blade relationship, followed by an attack.

Closing the line: Opposition

"Line" and "opposition" are not, as far as I am aware, 17th century fencing terms. However, they describe aspects of fencing that are truly universal, and are used extensively in the historical fencing community, so it is important that you know what they mean in this context.

Line, quite simply, refers to the path of blade to target, be that your blade to his target, or his to yours. If there is nothing obstructing the line between your sword and the target you wish to hit, in the path of the blow you wish to strike, then the line is open. If there is an obstruction, then the line is closed. It is obvious, then, that all attacks are made into an open or an opening line; and all defence relies (in part at least) on closing the line of the attack.

In this system the primary defence is opposition. This describes the relationship between your blades; if your forte is interposed between his debole and your body, you "have opposition". You can oppose his blade when stringering, when attacking, as a defence, indeed any time when you are in measure. If you think of the first half of your blade as your shield, and you always keep yourself covered by that shield, you have opposition.

Putting these two concepts together, you are have opposition when his line to your body is closed. Whenever you attack, if you do so with opposition, then you are safe because you have closed the line. Rapier fencing is, by and large, the art of manipulating your opponent until you have an open line and he has a closed one, so you can hit him safely.

Avoidance

Capo Ferro includes a range of avoidance actions in his system. You can avoid to either side, to the rear, or by going underneath the incoming sword. (The movie favourite of leaping over a cut to the legs is not recommended.) This is usually done as an alternative to opposition; in effect, by getting out of the way, you change the line to your body, such that he is no longer attacking in the right direction. Incidentally, avoidance actions are comparatively large, as they require you to move at least your front leg back (as in plate 8), or your entire body to the side (as in plates 17 and 19). They are therefore much slower than simply shifting your sword from one guard to another, and are consequently only usually done as part of a planned attack.

Defence in single time

The ideal defence with the rapier in this system is to move as little as possible; when your opponent moves (such as when attacking you), in one smooth motion you close the line and strike. Indeed, the majority of the primary techniques that Capo Ferro shows are single actions, be they attacks with opposition (when you set aside the incoming blade and strike in one action), or avoidances. By combining attack and defence into one smooth tempo, you make your opponent's defence much more difficult.

Defence in double time

There will be times when it is not possible to defend yourself in a single motion, and so instead you must expend one motion in defence (usually beating the attack aside), before striking in a second motion. This is easier for your opponent to deal with, but a marked improvement over getting hit, so it is a perfectly valid choice. It follows then that you should try to manipulate your opponent such that he is forced to act in two tempi as often as possible. The stringering is a good example of this in action.

Chapter 9

Next Step ... Free Play!

Building up your skills to the point that you can actually fence with someone and stay within the system is remarkably difficult. Under stress, your body will revert to instinctive responses, and the play becomes sloppy, unpredictable, and pointless. The trick is to train your responses with ever increasing pressure, and degrees of freedom, until you find yourself executing the techniques you know as cleanly in freeplay as you do in drill.

I have seen far too many fencers ruined by too much freeplay too soon: however much they may know in drill or theory, whenever it comes to a bout, they revert to opportunistic fencing, and their technique gets wilder and wilder as the bout progresses. The simple fact is that it is far better to get hit a lot and keep good form, than it is to never get hit in the salle but have poor form. In the first case one improves through practice; eventually you become very hard to hit, because your fencing is efficient, perfectly timed, and you are able to give clear signals, in effect lying persuasively to your opponent. In the second case the fencer falls apart whenever he meets someone who has been trained properly for long enough.

The drills below represent a typical progression of training one drill (the first from plate 7) from basic drill to freeplay. A similar progression can be made with any action.

Preparation drill one: Stringering

1. Stand on guard in *terza*.
2. Your partner enters into wide measure, stringering your sword on the inside (in *quarta*), with your point threatening your face.
3. You are threatened by the stringere, and as he enters, disengage, turns your hand to *seconda*, and thrust as in the striking according to the point drills.

That's the set-up. Now, you get to introduce one "realistic" element. If you perceive a tempo to strike you in as he is coming to stringer, you may do so. You may "snipe" at his arm, or take advantage of any lack of defensiveness in his guard as he comes into distance. Against your quick and accurate point, you may find his approach becomes far more "leaden sandalled", more cautious.

Preparation drill two: cavazione

1. Stand on guard in *terza*.
2. Your partner enters into wide measure, stringering your sword on the inside (in *quarta*), with your point threatening your face.
3. You are threatened by the stringere, and as he enters, disengage, turns your hand to *seconda*, and thrust as in the striking according to the point drills.
4. As your point approaches him, on his outside, he turns his hand to *seconda*, and directs his point to your left eye.

That's the standard play. Now, at step 3, you may choose one of three options:

1. disengage and thrust as before
2. disengage, beat his blade and thrust
3. counterattack in contratempo as in contratempo drill one (A or B).

if you choose 1, your partner continues as in the standard play. If 2, he should deceive your beat and thrust, or failing that, parry your thrust and riposte. If 3, he should withdraw his right foot a little, and parry you in *seconda*, striking you in the flank (as in the *scannatura* drills). You are in effect training your partner to respond to *what is there* not *what he expects*.

Once this is working well, throw in the feint that completes the plays of this plate. If you can convince him to counterattack, parry and hit him in a single tempo or in two tempi.

Now, pick a technique from those already executed within the drill (but don't tell your partner which one). Keeping only the degrees of freedom outlined above, make that technique happen. If it is on the part of the one stringering, do it when it is your turn to initiate. Does it rely on a certain response to the stringering? If so, then see what you can do to make sure he gives you only the one you want. Against any other, make sure there is no way he can hit you; cede distance, or avoid him, just bide your time until you have manoeuvred him into doing what you want.

Once that is working successfully for both of you, see if you can anticipate what it is your partner wants you to do, and give him that technique, and, knowing what he's likely to counter with, have your own counter prepared: this is the basis of the stringered person's feint you have already done above.

The stringering game

I use this drill in almost every class, at it teaches the basic concepts of tempo and measure in an intuitive and fun way. It starts with only one response to the stringering, which plays back and forth; once the game is under way, you gradually introduce more options, until in the end there are four choices: disengage and step away;[1] disengage and attack; disengage and counter-stringer; or attack into your stringering (this last only if he sees a clear weakness in your position).

Part one: the basic form

1. Both fencers stand on guard in *terza,* out of measure
2. Approach your partner carefully,
   to stringer him on the inside in *quarta.*
3. As you enter into measure, partner disengages with a step back
4. and he enters to counter-stringer your *quarta* with his *seconda.*
5. As he does so, disengage with a step back,
6. and re-enter, stringering in *quarta.*
7. Repeat steps 3—6 about a dozen times.

If your form deteriorates, stop and re-set immediately. Be sure to wait until your partner is truly committing to his stringering before you counter it, and as you stringer, be very careful to observe the correct blade relationship.

Part two: introducing choice for one partner

1. Repeat steps 1—4 of part one.
2. As your partner enters (step 4 above), either continue as before, or pre-empt him by turning your sword to *seconda* and stringering him as he comes in. Accompany this with a sidestep to the left.
3. Partner, now stringered on the outside, disengages with a step back,
4. and re-enters, stringering either on the inside (in *quarta*), or on the outside (in *seconda*) as the opportunity arises.
5. Counter his stringering as in step 2: either disengage, retire and re-enter; or sidestep and stringer directly.
6. Repeat freely from step 2 onwards.

Part three: choice extended to both partners

1. Repeat steps 1—3 of part two
2. At step 3, partner may respond to the stringering with the same options: either disengage, retire and re-enter; or sidestep and stringer directly.
3. Repeat freely.

Note that the drill should flow back and forth, with either fencer stringering and being countered, being stringered and countering.

Part four: more choices

By now you should have the basic idea of this drill, and be able to fluently stringer and counter-stringer. So we now introduce a third choice: disengage and strike.

1. Repeat the entire drill,
2. when either party is stringered, they may now choose to disengage and strike.
3. If any other option is chosen, the drill continues.
4. If the strike is made successfully, stop, re-set and start again.

Part five: counterattacking

You should start to notice patterns in your partner's choices; it should begin to be predictable whether he steps back, sidesteps, or attacks. There are numerous cues you can give him to persuade him to take one or the other option. If you want him to disengage, make sure the crossing-point of the blades is far enough towards his point that he has room to disengage easily. If you want him to attack, make sure he has an opening to do so. So, it's time to put that power of persuasion and prediction to work.

1. Repeat the entire drill,
2. when either party is stringered, they may choose to disengage and strike.
3. If they do so, counterattack as in the plays of plate 7 or 16.
4. If any other option is chosen, the drill continues.
5. If the initial strike or counterattack is made successfully, stop, re-set and start again.

After playing the stringering game for a few minutes, re-establish proper form by going through some plays carefully.

Do you see how complex this gets, how quickly? Only when these kinds of degrees of freedom are easily dealt with in the context of the system as you know it, should you start to introduce further degrees, such as allowing other responses to the stringering (such as the beat), playing with the distance, etc. Then repeat the entire process with every drill or play you know.

It is not the purpose of this book to teach you to defend yourself with the rapier against every kind of opponent. I have limited the scope so far to other serious students of Capo Ferro. However, I would recommend you to train the above exercises with as many different partners as possible, as everyone is unique in their responses and their judgement. Some will attack at the slightest provocation; others will let you stalk them until you are so close you can just stab them. Once you are comfortable with a range of responses, try the prophesy exercise:

Prophecy drill

This exercise is designed to give the experienced, technically proficient student a realistic idea of how far they can control the fight. It is vital to be completely honest with yourself.

Part one

1. Choose a decision-tree drill, such as preparation drill two, above.
2. Approach your partner, knowing that they have (in this example) three options as you stringer.
3. Decide which of the three you want them to do
4. Without telling them which one you want, enter to stringer.
5. Partner responds with one of their three options.
6. Notice whether they give you the one you want, or something else. If you got what you wanted, give yourself one point.
7. Repeat ten times from step 2.

If you scored the maximum 10 points, well done, you are a prophet! And you probably have a very predictable partner. 8 out of ten is very good; less than 6 do not attempt the next step, part two. Remember though, that if you had an 80% chance of surviving your trip to training, you'd probably quit. A 99% success rate in duelling means you're dead.

Part two

1. Repeat part one, steps 1—5
2. have a counter prepared.
3. If at step 5 you get what you wanted, use your prepared counter.
4. If you got it right, and your counter worked, score two points.
5. If you got it right and your counter failed
   but you didn't get hit, score one.
6. If you got it right and your counter failed
   and you got hit, score minus one.
7. If you got it wrong, counter anyway. If it works, score zero.
8. If you got it wrong, and your counter fails, score minus two.
9. Repeat ten times.

The maximum score is +20, the minimum, -20. Score less than +10, and do not freeplay. Now go do the same against lots of other people, and see how you do.

When going through the preparation exercises and playing the stringering game, keep a tally in your head. This will give you some idea of how you may create opportunities for yourself when fencing.

Fencing success is in part a balance between reaction and action. In the first place, a fencer's reactions should be trained to the point that they can immediately exploit any errors on their opponent's part, and are able to instinctively counter a surprise attack. But that is only half the story. This is a duelling art, and as such both parties meet at a pre-arranged time, in a pre-arranged place, with pre-arranged weapons. They start out of measure with drawn swords, and fight from there. So this art is really about creating the opportunity to strike safely. There should be no surprises, as you enter into measure you control your opponent's options to the point that you know in advance when, where and how they are going to move. You can then create the fight as you wish. One of the best rapier fencers I have fenced with so far is Gary Chelak, of the Tattershall School of Defence. I am faster by a margin, and reasonably experienced, but when we last fenced I managed to run my mask onto his point an absurd number of times simply because he knew exactly what I was going to do before I did it, and so was able to counter easily. Speed and strength are useless against a prophet!

Freeplay itself

This, for me, is the heart of the art. Well executed fencing is a joy to be a part of, whether you are scoring well or not. Equally, freeplaying too soon is damaging to your technical skill, and will ultimately stunt your progress. The exercises in this chapter should give you a fair idea of whether you are ready yet or not. If in doubt, try videoing yourselves going through the advanced drills. If you think it looks sloppy, if you notice serious technical flaws, you probably need more time in basic training before free fencing will be good for your development.

Afterword

I sometimes ask my students why they train, and so far the best answer I've got is this: "it adds years to my life and life to my years".

There is no doubt that regular swordsmanship training makes you fitter, stronger, and healthier. We train for the love of it, and so it also helps our emotional and mental health. That is all that really matters: that every practitioner is healthier and happier by partaking in this amazing activity.

The specifics of what we train are to my mind far less important. I have always been interested in being good at fighting, so for me the point of doing all this research is to divine better ways of using the weapon than I could make up myself. For others, the historical accuracy itself is far more interesting. And there are certainly those who have no real interest in the historical or martial accuracy of their techniques, but kit up and batter away for fun. To my mind, provided you are clear about what you are doing, and represent your activity to the general public accurately, it is ALL good stuff.

So, I have no doubt that there will be some readers who will dig out points where Capo Ferro appears to disagree with what I am putting forward in this interpretation. Good luck to them. Likewise, some will get fed up with all this pernickety detail and just start having swordfights. I've got no problem with that. I would just ask all readers to remember that this book is a work of interpretation designed to make a 400 year old system available to modern fencers of any stripe. As with all such confections, new material and new ideas will cause changes to my rapier method: in my opinion if you are practising exactly the same interpretation for more than a year, you've either got it perfect or are no longer involved in historical research.

So, take this method for what it is, and enjoy making something useful from it!

Acknowledgements

One of the greatest pleasures of this profession is the kindness and helpfulness of the community it serves, and the sense of common purpose between fellow instructors. In particular, this book owes much to the prior work, generously shared, of William Wilson and Jherek Swanger. Sean Hayes and Tom Leoni were also particularly helpful with overall criticisms and suggestions, and thanks also to Tom, and Steve Reich, for the use of the Fabris plates.

If you find this book well-presented and the photographs useful, then all credit is due to Ilkka Hartikainen, who acted as photographer, layout artist, and cover designer. I have been extraordinarily fortunate to have such a talented graphic designer to work with.

Scott Wilson made the series of gorgeous swords you see in the chapter on the weapon specially for this book, and photographed them. He has

also supplied 90% of the training rapiers used in my school over the last five years, while the research for this book was being carried out.

Craig Johnson custom-made the sweet swept hilt rapier you see in my hand in most of these pictures; it is the finest training rapier I have ever held.

Topi Mikkola has worked with me on the interpretation of Capo Ferro's method since the beginning; I have lost track of how many details of execution come from his observations and suggestions.

The following people also contributed their expert knowledge in design, content editing and/or proof-reading the manuscript in various stages: Stephen Hand, Allen Reed, Greg Mele, Claire Falcon, and Chris Blakey.

My students, who have put up with revision after revision of the basic method, and continue to challenge and inspire me to yet more training and research.

To all of the above, kiitos paljon!

Thanks above all are due to my beloved Michaela, who puts up with a workaholic writer/swordsman with every appearance of love and patience.

In a Nutshell

Points to remember

In the Salle

1. **Safety:** safety first! Never hit anyone by accident or in anger.
2. **Respect:** for the Art, your training partners, and the weapon. This is demonstrated by courtesy.

When fencing

1. **Do not get hit.**
2. **Hit, but only when you can still obey the first rule.**

Fundamentals

1. **Precision:** Never sacrifice your precision.
   Pay special attention to your guard position, measure, and the relationship between the blades.
2. **Line:** Keep your lines closed, open his. This is done by always retaining opposition: keep your forte between his debole and you.
3. **Leverage:** only oppose strength to weakness; if he has a leverage advantage, retreat while changing the blade relationship.

Tempo

1. **Movement:** when he moves, that's a tempo: hit him!
2. **Stillness:** when he stays still, that's a tempo: hit him!
3. **Shorter is better:** make sure your tempo is shorter and therefore faster than his.

Tactics

1. **Tempo:** ensure that you need fewer, shorter tempi to strike than he does.
2. **Caution:** safety first: always maintain opposition
3. **Prophecy:** manipulate measure, tempo and line so you know when and where he'll move, and as he does so, hit him!

Techniques

1. **Counterattack:** against an attack, counterattack.
2. **Parry:** against an attack or counterattack, parry.
3. **Disengage:** when the leverage is against you, disengage.
4. **Opening line:** only attack an opening line, or to create an opening line.
5. **Avoid:** avoid when possible, stepping away from blade contact.

Troubleshooting

If a technique is not working, the problem always lies in one or more of the
following areas:

1. **Distance:** are you in the right place to do it?
2. **Timing:** is there a tempo to do it in?
3. **Configuration:** hand position, opposition,
   point control, are they right?
4. **Direction:** are you going in the right
   direction for the technique in question?

Appendix 2

Joint Safety

Here are a few simple guidelines for joint safety, which should be followed during all training. I am using the lunge as an example of a stressful action, but these principles apply to any physical action.

- The knee must always bend in the line of the foot. Knees are hinges, with usually a little under 180° range of movement. The do not respond well to torque (power in rotation). So whenever you bend your knees, in any style for any reason, ensure that the line of your foot, the line of movement of your knee, and the line of movement of your weight, are parallel. This prevents twisting and thus injuries. This one simple rule, carefully followed, eliminates all knee problems other than those arising from impact or genetic disadvantage.
- Whenever performing any strenuous task (such as lunging, or lifting televisions), **tighten your pelvic floor muscles (imagine you need to go to the bathroom, but are stuck in a queue).** This supports the base of your spine, and helps with hip alignment.
- Joints have two forms of support: active and passive. Passive support refers mainly to the ligaments, which bind the joint capsule together. This is basically set, and can't be trained. When training your joint strength, with exercises or stretching, avoid any action that strains the joint capsule. Any action that causes pain in the joint itself should **be modified or avoided as it may damage the soft tissues (ligaments, tendons, cartilage).** These tissues have a very poor blood supply and hence heal very slowly.
- Active support refers to the muscles around the joint, and these can be strengthened by carefully straining the joint with small weights and rotations. To strengthen a joint you must stress these muscles, without endangering the ligaments. Any competent physiotherapist can show you a range of exercises for building up the active support around your knees, wrists and elbows, where we need it most.
- Rest is part of training. Your body needs time to recover, and is stimulated by the stress of exercise to grow stronger. However, the **body is efficient and will withdraw resources from any muscle group** that is not used, even if for only a few weeks. So regular training is absolutely crucial.

If you can't lunge without warming up, don't lunge except in carefully controlled drills. Warming up is essential before pushing the boundaries of what your body can do, but before considering freeplay where the lunge might be used you should condition yourself to the point where you can get out of bed in the morning and immediately do 10 full lunges, full speed, without risk of strain or injury.

Training Schedule

This is lifted in part from my previous work, but it bears repeating here. The structure of your ideal training schedule will change as you become more proficient, but to get the most out of this book, I would advise that you practise along these lines.

Firstly, establish regular training times. Ideally this should be two hours a day, but in the real world, with non-professional swordsmen, it is more likely to be once or twice a week. Once you have established your schedule, stick to it. In general, little and often is better for re-programming muscle memory than an occasional 8-hour mega-session.

The method in this book is laid out in the order that you should practice: warm-up, body-mechanics, footwork, solo sword practice, pair exercise, freeplay. Do not expect to cover everything in one session, and do not try to do every exercise of each type each time. Progress gradually through the exercises in the order that they are written.

The first set of 8 sessions should look like this:

1. Warm-up: 10—15 minutes.
2. Conditioning exercises: 20—30 minutes.
3. Footwork exercises: 20—30 minutes.
4. Solo sword practice: 20—30 minutes.
5. Finish with a warm-down emphasising stretches.

Then, depending on how well you have mastered the basic solo practice, the second set of 8 sessions should go like this:

1. warm-up: 10—15 minutes.
2. conditioning exercises: 15—20 minutes.
3. footwork exercises: 15—20 minutes.
4. solo sword practice: 20—30 minutes.
5. pair exercises: 20—30 minutes.
6. Finish with a warm-down emphasising stretches.

Increase the amount of time spent on pair exercises in the third set of 8 sessions:

1. Warm-up: 10—15 minutes.
2. Conditioning exercises: 10—15 minutes.
3. Footwork exercises: 10—15 minutes.
4. Solo sword practice: 10—15 minutes.
5. Pair exercises: 30—40 minutes.
6. Finish with a warm-down emphasising stretches.

When you are comfortable with all the pair exercises introduce the freeplay preparation exercises into about two training sessions in four. To counterbalance the detrimental effect that faster, more random practice has on your basic, core technique, reintroduce more basic solo training to your schedule, both immediately after the more advanced exercises, and in subsequent sessions, so in any four sessions you will have two including freeplay preparation, one from the second set, and one from the third. So the fourth set of 8 sessions will go something like this:

First session

1. Warm-up: 10—15 minutes.
2. conditioning exercises: 10—15 minutes.
3. Footwork exercises: 10—15 minutes.
4. Solo sword practice: 10—15 minutes.
5. Pair exercises: 20—30 minutes.
6. Freeplay preparation: 10 minutes.
7. Slow pair exercises: 10 minutes.
8. Finish with a warm-down emphasising stretches.

Second session

1. Warm-up: 10—15 minutes.
2. conditioning exercises: 15—20 minutes.
3. Footwork exercises: 15—20 minutes.
4. Solo sword practice: 20—30 minutes.
5. Pair exercises: 20—30 minutes.
6. Finish with a warm-down emphasising stretches.

Third session

1. Warm-up: 10—15 minutes.
2. conditioning exercises: 10—15 minutes.
3. Footwork exercises: 10—15 minutes.
4. Solo sword practice: 10—15 minutes.
5. Pair exercises: 20—30 minutes.
6. Freeplay preparation: 10 minutes.
7. Slow pair exercises: 10 minutes.
8. Finish with a warm-down emphasising stretches.

Fourth session

1. Warm-up: 10—15 minutes.
2. conditioning exercises: 10—15 minutes.
3. Footwork exercises: 10—15 minutes.
4. Solo sword practice: 10—15 minutes.
5. Pair exercises: 30—40 minutes.
6. Finish with a warm-down emphasising stretches.

Repeat the pattern to make eight sessions.

Then we introduce freeplay (if you feel you're ready for it; do not be rushed into it), towards the end of every other session, so that in the next set of eight sessions there will be four including freeplay, two where you go back to basics, and two where you focus on pair drills.

The above schedule covers 40 two-hour sessions. Once you have practised that much you should have a fair idea where your weaknesses are, and you will find that the solution to those weaknesses will be found in one or other of the basic drills. So adjust your schedule to fit your own needs (and those of your training partner or group), to work on the aspects of swordsmanship you find most difficult. You may find it useful to keep a record of when and what you have practised. Remember that *every* session should include a warm-up, basic footwork exercises, basic solo sword-handling exercises, and a warm-down.

Notes

Introduction

1. The title in full: *Scola overo teatro nel qual sono rappresentate diverse mainiere e modi di parare et di ferire di spada sola, e di spada e pugnale*, by Niccolo Giganti, Venice 1606.

2. *Scienza e practica d'arme*, Copenhagen 1606.

3. This and all other English language quotations are from Jherek Swanger and William Wilson's fine translation, available online. However, all serious students of the rapier should also refer to Jared Kirby's *Italian Rapier Combat*, a translation of the *Gran Simulacro*, including beautiful plates. All proceeds from sales of Kirby's book go to a fund for providing further translations of historical fencing manuals.

4. Such as Table, 93 : "The *passatas* [advancing by passing the left foot forwards] are not good, because they lose measure and tempo…" despite plates 9,11,12,13, 18, 20, 33, 34, 40, and 41 clearly showing them (and they occur in several other unillustrated plays).

5. Strictly speaking, Agrippa defines the guard by the position of the hand relative to the body, not the degree of rotation of the hand (palm up, palm to the left, etc.) that Capo Ferro is using, and that survives to this day.

Chapter 1

1. Joachim Meyer: *Gründtliche Beschreibung der […] kunst des Fechtens […]* Strassburg, 1570. His method describes a completely different system to Capo Ferro's, emphasising cutting actions. Meyer's sword is almost certainly a little shorter, and with a broader blade.

2. Published in 1980

3. Published in 1980

4. Fought over German territory, from 1618 to 1648.

5. See pages 163 to 165 of *European Weapons and Armour*

Chapter 4

1. Scienza e practica d'arme, Copenhagen 1606. I was unconvinced by the utility of this position until I saw William Wilson demonstrate it at ISMAC, Lansing, 2001, and further by seeing Tom Leoni use it against me in free fencing at The Schola St George Medieval Swordsmanship Symposium, Benecia 2003.

2. Where period typeface differs from modern usage, I have attempted to duplicate it, so readers unfamiliar with the source will get a flavour of it.

3. This and all other Italian language quotations are from the original treatise, the 1610 edition of Ridolfo Capo Ferro da Cagli's Gran Simulacro dell'arte e dell'uso della Scherma, available online.

4. Which Capo Ferro defines in Explanations 3 (p. 34) "when at the very same time that the adversary wants to strike me, I encounter him in shorter tempo and measure".

5. Hunter Textbooks, 1987. I am further indebted to Mro. Hayes, who gave me his copy of this now hard-to-get book.

6. I was confused at first by this statement: "The crossing of the left foot toward the right side in performing an inquartata is worthless; it can make of itself a shortcoming, because it hinders the body and shortens the motion of the right arm in striking, with loss of tempo". (Table, 92) The inquartata is, as implied in this excerpt, a defensive action, common to all Italian rapier styles, in which you pass your left foot behind you to the right, to get out of the way of your opponent's sword, usually while striking him. This is apparently the same as the scanso della vita, which on plate 19 is described as being performed "with a void of the body by stepping with the left leg crossing behind the right". The solution to this apparent contradiction lies in the degree to which the leg is allowed to cross: the picture on plate 19 clearly shows the defender, C, gaining distance with the scanso; hence there is no "shortcoming". This was pointed out to me by John O'Meara, a rapier instructor with the Chicago Swordplay Guild, in conversation at ISMAC in Lansing, August 2004.

7. This is apparently almost identical to Agrippa's "Atto G", a position taken when avoiding to the right.

8. Capo Ferro does not name this action: I call it sbasso because the duck-hit is often called that in other Italian fencing systems, and it is easier to teach a move when it has a simple name.

9. See page 24 of Forgeng's excellent The Medieval Art of Swordsmanship, Chivalry Bookshelf 2003.

10. See *Flos Duellatorum*, **carta 20B, lower left figure. Michelini translates the** accompanying text as: When one wants to hit your leg with the sword, / Strike his head or his throat; / Or hit the arms rather the head, Because the distance is shorter.

Chapter 5

1. This is perhaps a nod to Agrippa who assigns every position in his treatise a letter.

2. This is a description of how it feels; anatomists and physicists may argue that the front leg actually does the work. However, to execute the recovery swiftly and easily, it should feel that you pull yourself back.

3. Refer to The Swordsman's Companion, pp 82 to 84 for a discussion on the physics of cutting.

4. On page 57 Verso.

5. I am indebted to Tom Leoni who explained this to me in conversation, in Racine, September 2004

Chapter 6

1. Florio translates "palmo" as "a spanne, a shaftsman, a handsbreadth". The closest thing to a precise modern measurement available is given by the Oxford English Dictionary, which defines a "span" as "the maximum distance between the tips of the thumb and the little finger" (which for me is 8¼ inches, 21 cm), and as "a measurement, equal to 9 inches" (22.9 cm).

2. My interpretation of stringere in particular owes much to the work of Sean Hayes, Tom Leoni, and Jherek Swanger.

3. Not to be confused with stringare: "to point [as in to tie with 'points', like modern laces], or trusse with points. Also to mince or wire-draw a thing. Also to stand upon strict points. Also to bang or ribbaste one". (Florio 540)

4. Florio's Dictionary of 1611 translates the term as: "to binde, to wrinch, to guird in, to claspe, to clinch, to pinch, to straiten, to wring in. Also to urge, to force or constraine unto". (Florio 540). Capo Ferro also expresses the concept in two other ways: guadagnar, ("to gaine, to winne, to profit, to get, to acquire. Also to deserve", Florio 222), and acquistare ("to acquire, to purchase", Florio 9). Greg Lindahl's online version can be found at *http://www.pbm.com/~lindahl/florio/*

5. By G.A., author's full name unknown.

6. Because the term was anglicised so long ago, it is correct practice to leave it un-italicised when used as an English word.

7. It was standard practice in Viking times to describe a sword as if it is hanging point-down, a tradition continued by Ewart Oakeshott, and discussed by him on page 127 of European Weapons and Armour. He notes that modern scholars generally describe swords as seen point-up. I however will follow Oakeshott (who better?).

8. Translated by Tommaso Leoni and published by Chivalry Bookshelf in 2005 under the title *Art of Duelling*. This is an *excellent* resource, and a must-read for all students of Italian rapier.

9. I am indebted to Gary Chelak for pointing this out to me in conversation, 8th October 2005.

10. I have standardised this spelling; Capo Ferro uses the more archaic form "*cavatione*".

11. Some modern practitioners refer to this position as "terza outside the knee". While a perfectly valid choice, I would not want to give the impression that Capo Ferro uses this term, so I avoid it here.

12. I have once put my weapon 4" into my friend's thigh, while fencing with a borrowed weapon that I would not pass as safe for fencing in my salle (too rigid, and with no button on the point). As I attacked to his (well protected) chest, he parried down with his left hand while passing forward. My lunge and his pass provided sufficient force to send my round but unbuttoned point through his jeans, and through the skin of his thigh. The point passed between skin and muscle within an inch of his femoral artery, and while my sword was in his leg, he hit me in the chest. However, my sword came out so easily that it was actually three days before we realised what had happened; there was no bleeding, and it was only when the bruising came up on the back of his leg that he went to the hospital to get it checked. Anecdotal evidence is not proof, but there are also innumerable examples in the literature of people hitting back after receiving stab wounds.

13. Capo Ferro spells this term "cavatione"; I have modernised the spelling for convenience only.

14. Florio does not give this term, but the verb it is derived from, *cavare*, he translates as "to dig, to make hollow, to draw out from, to cave, to mine". He goes on to list eleven phrases that use it, including *cavare sangue*, to draw blood. Florio, 90

15. I was shown this alternative by Gary Chelak in October 2005, and have been using it ever since.

16. My student Topi Mikkola interprets this play differently, with a corkscrew motion of the sword parrying with the false edge and spiralling into an imbroccata in one action; this interpretation would be an example of contratempo.

17. In the original sequence, the stringerer counterattacks with a pass, grasping the opponent's sword hand. I made a mistake during the photoshoot and had Rami lunge instead. So the text has been modified to fit the pictures. The play works fine this way, but is not as Capo Ferro specifies. The error was unfortunately spotted too late to reshoot.

Chapter 8

1. Readers of my first book, *The Swordsman's Companion*, will notice a difference; there I describe the four aspects of any technique as time, distance configuration and direction. Those four aspects are still at work with the rapier, but given the extensive theory explanations given by Capo Ferro, it would be misleading and unnecessary to use them here. Configuration and Direction are both represented here by "line".

2. Again, thanks are due to Mr. Swanger: his translation of Viggiani is excellent. See for further details pages 63 Recto through 64 Verso where Viggiani defines tempo.

3. Note the variant spellings of "*mezo*"; Viggiani uses *mezo*, Capo Ferro, *mezzo*.

Chapter 9

1. Though this action is recommended by capo Ferro in Table 111 as the most sensible response to being stringered, it is entirely absent from the plays. Notice, though, that in those plays where a fencer disengages and strikes immediately, he is normally countered by the stringerer. It seems a necessary skill, and if you find yourself stringered and think your attack may fail, it is the most sensible option. This game and my incorporation of the disengage-step back action in it are a direct result of a long conversation held after my rapier class at WMAW 2005 with David Biggs (who brought the subject up), William Wilson, and Stephen Reich.

Bibliography

Fencing treatises

Fabris, Salvator, *Scienza e pratica d'arme* (1606)

Fiore de' Liberi da Premariacco, *Flos Duellatorum in armis, sine armis, equester, pedester ed.* (1409) ed. Francesco Novati (1902) (the Pisani-Dossi manuscript).

Fiore dei Liberi da Premariacco, *Fior Battaglia* (c.a.1410) (the Getty manuscript).

Filippo di Vadi, *De Arte Gladiatoria Dimicandi* (c.a. 1482—1487)

Anonymous, Royal Armouries Manuscript I.33, (c.a.1295)

G.A. (author's full name not known), *Pallas Armata* (1639)

dall'Agocchie, Giovanni, *Dell'arte di scrimia libri tre* (1572)

Alfieri, Francesco Ferdinando, *La Scherma* (1640)

Capoferro, Ridolfo, *Gran simulacro dell'arte e dell'uso della scherma* (1610)

di Grassi, Giacomo, *Ragione di adoprar...*(1570). English translation *Giacomo di Grassi, his true Arte of defence,* etc. (1594)

Manciolino, Antonio, *Opera Nova ...* (1531)

Marozzo, Achille, *Opera Nova ...* (1536)

Saviolo, Vincento, *His Practice* (1595)

Viggiani, Angelo, *Lo schermo* (1575)

Translations

Michelini, Hermes, unpublished translation of *Flos duellatorum.*

Porzio, Luca, and Mele, Gregory, *Arte Gladiatoria Dimicandi: 15th Century Swordsmanship of Filippo Vadi,* Chivalry Bookshelf (2003)

Forgeng, Jeffrey L., *The Medieval Art of Swordsmanship: A Facsimile & Translation of Europe's Oldest Personal Combat Treatise, Royal Armouries MS 1.33* Chivalry Bookshelf (2003)

Swanger, Jherek, and Wilson, William; unpublished translation of Capo Ferro's *Gran Simulacro*

Kirby, Jared, *Italian Rapier Combat* (translation of *Gran Simulacro*) Greenhill Books, 2004

Leoni, Tommaso, *Art of Duelling, Salvatore Fabris' rapier fencing treatise of 1606*, Chivalry Bookshelf, 2005

Other reference works

Anglo, Sydney, *The Martial Arts of Renaissance Europe* (Yale University Press, 2000).

Florio, John, *Queen Anna's New World of Wordes, or Dictionarie*, 1611

Hand, Stephen (ed.) *SPADA Anthology of Swordsmanship* (Chivalry Bookshelf 2002)

Gaugler, William M., *Fencing Everyone*, Hunter Textbooks 1987

Scherger, John S., The Study of Human Movement by the Application of Biomechanical Muscular Leverage Physics: Understanding the Effective Lever Arm, online at http://www.spinalfitness.com/Demo/effective%20lever%20arms.PDF (accessed June 1st 2006)

CPSIA information can be obtained at www.ICGtesting.com
Printed in the USA
BVOW03s1609051214

377971BV00033B/1155/P